FROM RUSSIA WITH JOKES

How to Be a Successful Public Speaker When You Don't Speak English

Matvei Finkel

Russian-American Island

Published by Russian-American Island

Copyright © 1992 by Matvei Finkel

Co-author & Editor: John F. Carter

Cover Design: Chris Bishop

Photo of St. Basil's Cathedral by Sergei Petrov

All rights reserved. No part of this book may be reproduced in any form or by any means without the prior written consent of the publisher.

First Printing: February, 1992
10 9 8 7 6 5 4 3 2 1

Library of Congress Catalog Card Number: 91-068219

ISBN: 0-9631688-1-9

1. Finkel, Matvei. 2. Russia -- Soviet Union. 3. Jokes -- Humor. 4. Public Speaking.

Printed in the United States of America

Contents

Introduction -- What A Country!   5

Chapter 1 -- "Crazy People Will Pay Money To Listen To You!"   7
    How I Left Russia And Lived To Tell About It: Leonid Brezhnev, Walter Cronkite, The Toilet

Chapter 2 -- To Be Successful, Keep Your Mouth Shut   11
    The Goals Of Public Speaking: Inform, Entertain, Persuade

Chapter 3 -- How Many Bullets For A Joke?   15
    Using Humor In Presentations: Jokes, Funny Stories

Chapter 4 -- Don't Be Surprised   19
    Memorizing The Speech: A Brief Example, Mini Speeches And Main Points, Dramatic Endings

Chapter 5 -- Who Discovered America?   22
    Practice Makes Perfect: Visualize Success, Key Words, Rehearsal, Storytelling

Chapter 6 -- Always Keep Your Mouth Wet   26
    Body Language: Calm Your Nerves, Warm Up Your Voice, Wear A Smile... And Clothes

Chapter 7 -- Don't Laugh, This Is Russia!   30
    Final Preparations And Beginning A Presentation: Arrive Early, Set The Stage, Build Rapport, The First Five Minutes, The Explanation, The Results

Chapter 8 -- Fool Them All By Refusing To Shut Up   35
    Timing, Breaks And Questions: The Beginning, Why And When To Break, The End, Handling Questions, Encourage Your Listeners

Chapter 9 -- The Russians Are Coming! 39
    Research: Observe, Listen, Get Involved, What I Learned

Chapter 10 -- Secret Ballots And Other Mysteries 42
    Speaking Of History And Current Events: Help Them Remember, Tell Stories, Give Credit, Reaching A Conclusion

Chapter 11 -- Matvei In The Lions Den 46
    Speaking To Different Audiences: Finding The Right Places, Learn Something New, Surrounded

Chapter 12 -- Russian Life Is No Game 51
    Speaking At Schools: Play Games, Catch Their Interest, Back To The New Russia, Boris Yeltsin, The Problems, Models

Chapter 13 -- Speech Is Free, Audience Is Extra 58
    Getting Invited To Speak: Reputation, The Search, Letters, Flyers, Brochures, Recommendations, Contracts

Chapter 14 -- From Russia With More Jokes 61
    Humor You Can Use: Communism, Economics, Militarism And The K.G.B., Gorbachev, Vodka, Shortages, Yeltsin, Free Market Blues, Political Change

Appendix 70

"Anyone can be a public speaker in America, and if you can tell a few jokes, you can be vice president like Dan Quayle."
-- Advice from a Democratic Party Leader to Matvei Finkel

Introduction

What A Country!

The best speakers draw on their own experience to take their listeners places they have never been. They tell captivating stories that entertain as they inform. And most of all, they never stop being curious about the world around them.

I have lived in two very different, very curious worlds. Sometimes I think my former life in Moscow happened not just on another continent, but on another planet.

The Russia I left four years ago was a land of paradoxes. There was no unemployment, but no one worked; no one worked, but productivity went up; productivity went up, but there was nothing in the stores; there was nothing in the stores, but at home there was everything; at home there was everything, but no one was satisfied; no one was satisfied, but everyone voted "Yes."

The Russia I left was still wedded to Socialist Realism, an oxymoron. This led millions of Soviet workers to tell their superiors pleasant things they liked to hear, using simple words they could understand.

It was an unworkable empire where knowledge brought depression, or repression, rather than power. Optimists, it was said, were poorly informed pessimists, and pessimists were fully informed optimists.

The Russia I left had more food lines than food, more people than apartments to house them, more talk of freedom than freedom to talk. It had no parking problems because cars were so hard to get, and no garbage problems because people used everything they got their hands on. Its capital city, Moscow, resembled Gotham City before Batman cleaned it up.

The Russia I left specialized in Catch-22 situations. My applications for a visa to go to the West was denied because I knew a state secret. "But in my field of science, the USSR is 10 years behind the West," I complained. "This is the state secret that you know," was the reply.

This was the place I left four years ago, and if I spend my time speaking about it to groups of people in a distant land, it is only because Russia still occupies my thoughts and memories with a firmer grip than it wields over its own discontented citizens. That is why I became a public speaker. I had to tell people about this strange place.

But not everyone believes me. Like the student at South Puget Sound Community College who challenged me with the following question.

"Mr. Finkel, do you work for the KGB or the CIA?" "Neither," I answered. "If I worked for the CIA, I would charge you more. If I worked for the KGB, I would have a better accent."

The best Russian jokes are not born in comedy clubs, but in lines. Indeed,

Russians spend half their lives in line: they are born in line, they die in line (not enough hospital beds), they eat in line, buy soap in line, and, of course, they joke in line.

When I decided to become a public speaker, I asked a professional speaker if I needed to include jokes in my presentations. "Only if you want to get paid," he replied.

What a country!

My first lesson on radiating a smile at an audience I received from President Jimmy Carter in July 1987.

Chapter 1

"Crazy People Will Pay Money to Listen To You!"

(How I Left Russia And Lived To Tell About It)

I have a career as a speaker thanks to three important influences on my life: Leonid Brezhnev, Walter Cronkite and the toilet.

Leonid Brezhnev

I know a lot of people are surprised at how Leonid Brezhnev, who died in 1982 and was general secretary of the Communist Party, helped me. Maybe he was my teacher.

Brezhnev, as other Soviet party leaders, didn't know how to speak. A classic example is the presentation he gave during the beginning of the 1980 Olympic Games in Moscow. You may not remember, since the United States didn't participate over the war in Afghanistan.

> At the Olympics ceremony Brezhnev opened a book -- all party leaders are supposed to read their speeches -- and he started by saying, "O - O - O - O - O," the same sound five times. Finally the guy behind him said, "Comrade Brezhnev, that's not your speech. Your speech is on the second page. That is the Olympic symbol."

One interesting thing about the way Brezhnev spoke: he was loosing his teeth. No one could understand what he was talking about, but people were afraid to ask him.

How did he help me? In 1977, I met a girl from the United States -- the first American I met in my life. It was a terribly rainy day, and my mother invited her into our apartment and gave her my blue jeans to wear while hers dried. When I came home from work and found this girl in my blue jeans, I was very upset, because those were the only jeans I had. To buy them, I had spent most of my salary.

> To give you an idea of how important jeans are in Soviet life, a wealthy man went to the dentist. He asked the dentist to replace his teeth with the most expensive thing he could find. The dentist said, "Do you want golden teeth?" "No," said the man, "I'm rich." "Do you want diamond teeth?" asked the dentist. "No, don't you understand," said the man. "I'm really rich. I want denim teeth!"

Jeans were very important, but they didn't keep me from marrying this girl. After I did that, I lost my job. Our wedding in 1979 was just two weeks before the Soviet military occupied Afghanistan. Americans were enemies of Russians, and my neighbors started to call me an American spy. Why? Because in the Soviet Union it's not necessary to be smart or produce anything to be successful. You just have to keep your mouth shut. I was different because my wife was an American. I lost my job as an aircraft engineer -- who wants to hire an American spy? This was all during Brezhnev's time.

You can say, "It's okay not to have a job. A lot of people in the United States don't have a job." But in the Soviet Union it was against the law to be unemployed. If you were unemployed for more than a year, the government would send you to a labor camp. So you had to find a job!

Finally, I found a job with the help of my friends and started working for CBS News. I was a liaison person, a driver, a soundman -- I did everything. I thank Brezhnev for helping to launch my career as a speaker by forcing me to work for an American television network.

Walter Cronkite

"Wait a minute," you are thinking, "he's not a speaker yet." But one day while working for CBS News, I received an order to go to the airport to meet a very important person. This person happened to be Walter Cronkite. Of course I didn't know who he was, but as soon as I met him I found he was a very nice person; like a grandfather, only very intelligent and sophisticated.

I told him about my problems. That my wife was pregnant and the KGB was after me, and he decided to help. He introduced me to Armand Hammer and other officials. He also gave me a feeling of self-esteem. One time after a very successful shooting, he invited me to a Japanese restaurant that was the most expensive in the Soviet Union. At the restaurant, he asked me what I was going to do with my life in the future. I said, "If it's possible, I will go to the United States and maybe I will be an engineer again."

"I don't think you can be an engineer," he said. "You've been out of school for a long time. I'm making a film about the Soviet economy. It's about 20 years behind the American economy, so we have different tools."

He didn't want to offend me, but I understood what he was saying. "So what do you think I can do," I asked. "I don't have any other skills and I don't know what I'll do."

He said, "When you go to the United States, just tell people about your life."
"Who's interested in my life?" I replied.

"Oh," he laughed, "in the United States you will find plenty of crazy people who will pay money just to go and listen to you."

I didn't get a chance to find out any more about this great idea, because just then a Russian waiter (they had Russian waiters in the Japanese restaurant) poured soy sauce on my jacket. We started to argue with him about cleaning my jacket, and our conversation got sidetracked.

The next day when I came to the hotel to pick up Walter Cronkite, I wanted to find out more about my new career. My mother had always said to keep my mouth shut; it would help me to survive. Now I was going to talk in public, and I wanted to pump more information out of Mr. Cronkite.

When I met him, he was upset about something. Since it wasn't a good time to talk about my new career, I asked him why he was upset.

"It's funny," he said, "but somebody stole my pants. I was shooting yesterday in Red Square and my pants got dirty. I gave them to a lady at the hotel to clean them so I could wear them today to finish the filming, and now I can't find them."

My first thought was that his pants had come back from the cleaners and were somewhere in his room. My mother used to say that if you lost something, look in a crack. Most Soviet apartments are just full of cracks between panels in the walls and floors. But I looked at Walter Cronkite, who is a pretty big man, and I knew it was practically impossible to find a crack in the Soviet Union big enough for his pants.

After a couple of hours, Mr. Cronkite came to the conclusion that the KGB, the Soviet secret police, didn't like the show he was making on the lousy Soviet economy. So to stop him from shooting, they stole his pants. Two days later he found them in one of his suitcases, but for two days he was proudly telling everyone, "The KGB stole my pants."

The Toilet

I thank Brezhnev and Cronkite for helping launch my career, but I have to give credit to the toilet for really making me a high-profile public speaker.

In September 1987, two weeks after I moved to the United States, I received a call from the Society Against Malicious Harassment. Since I am Jewish, married to an American, and had been trying to leave the Soviet Union for eight years, they figured I knew a thing or two about being harassed. They invited me to a dinner and offered to pay for my dinner if I would speak for just two minutes.

If these people will give me dinner, maybe next time I could give a presentation for money, I thought. I needed money; when I left the Soviet Union I had only $104 in my pocket. I had an eight-month old daughter and a wife with three diplomas and no job. The first job I found was delivering pizza. It wasn't great, but it did help me learn how to communicate with people to receive more tips. I started to write some sentences before going on a delivery, like "Russian delivery man with pizza." It was very simple English, but I did receive more tips than the other guys.

So I went to the Malicious Harassment dinner and earned a reputation as a public speaker that I'm still trying to live down. This human rights organization was leading the fight against a nearby compound of unrepentant racists, so the tables at this banquet held representatives of most every skin color available to the human race. Blacks, American Indians, Hispanics, Asians and Anglos filled the chairs, waiting for me to give them some thoughts on the dangers of intolerance and the glories of freedom.

It was a long wait. Having finished their meal, most of the people were engaged in conversation and the master of ceremonies at the head table seemed content to let this continue for a while longer. I joined in the discussion, all of the while drinking wine and coffee until I felt a distinct need to find a men's room.

The buzz of conversation ended, of course, as soon as I slipped out of the hall. Minding my own business in the men's room, I began to notice the sound of frantic voices drifting through the air ducts. "Where is he?" "Look in there!" "Find him for goodness sake!!!"

Just then a woman burst through the men's room door, grabbed my shoulders from behind, and shouted "You've got to speak right now!" in a half-crazed voice.

I was so embarrassed, that afterwards I thought it was the last time anyone would ask me to speak. Imagine my surprise when several days later I received a call from a man asking if I would speak to another group.

"How did you find out about me?" I asked.

"It was easy," he replied. "Everybody's talking about the speaker from the toilet!"

Chapter 2

"To Be Successful, Keep Your Mouth Shut!"

(The Goals Of Public Speaking)

"Keep your mouth shut." That was my mother's advice when I was growing up in Russia, so public speaking didn't come naturally to me. After my infamous toilet speech, I started looking for books about public speaking. I found some that had useful techniques and others with jokes which I promptly stole for my own talks, but the most valuable thing I gleaned from these library books was the goal -- actually three goals -- of public speaking.

Inform

The first goal is to give information. When I arrived in the United States, I was immediately considered an expert on Russian life by virtue of having lived in it for more than 30 years. My knowledge of Russian culture was a commodity, like sausages or software, that people would pay to receive. When you are considered an expert on a country in upheaval, that can be valuable knowledge.

Most Americans who visit Russia don't realize it is a Third World country, since they stay in plush hotels designed by French architects and built by Yugoslavian construction workers. The first thing I tell anyone who says they are going to visit Russia is to stay with a Russian family. "Talk with the people, visit the hospitals," I say, "and be sure to use real Russian toilet paper. Then you will get a feel for life in that country."

Giving advice is easy for me. In my position as a lecturer on Russia at Whitworth College, my goal is to give information that people want. I also teach Russian classes, so I try to prepare every audience I address with the two most important words in the Russian language: "nyet" and "da." In Russia, people like to say nyet in response to everything. Lately they have been learning to say da more often, but it's still in second place. I have the people practice saying them after me, and then I give examples of how they are used in the Soviet Union.

> "If a Russian military officer says nyet, it means nyet," I explain. "If he says da, it's da. If a military officer says maybe, he's not a military officer." "If a Russian politician says da, it's maybe," I say. "If he says maybe, it's nyet. If a politician says nyet, he's not a politician."

11

Entertain

Conveying information about another culture or teaching vocabulary is a valuable service, but it's not the only goal of public speaking. A second goal is to entertain your audience. From a practical standpoint, the best way to get invited for more speaking dates is to make your presentation entertaining.

Russian bureaucrats never had to learn this lesson. The Communist Party leadership, at least until Gorbachev came along, felt that if a speech full of endless statistics didn't convince people that things were getting better, at least it would be so boring that no one would ask them any questions.

It's not only the bureaucrats either. Most Russian speakers try to give as much information as possible -- names, dates, quantities -- expecting their audience will memorize every word of it.

> **It's like the case of an American travelling in Russia who was lost. He stopped a Russian teacher on the street who spoke English, and asked her if she would help him find the place he was headed. "Yes," said the lady, and then she launched into a very fast explanation of directions that lasted ten minutes. The American realized his mistake, and when she finished, he just said, "Thank you very much." "Don't thank me yet," warned the teacher. "First you have to repeat it back to me."**

Russian education is boring. Every fact must be memorized, no matter how insignificant, and I wanted to make sure my speeches were not like that. So I set entertaining my audience as a goal. That doesn't mean I'm only an entertainer. I've just found that the best way to get information across to people is to present it in an entertaining manner. I tell stories that illustrate the points I want to make in my speech. I toss in a few jokes that point out the differences between cultures. And I get people from the audience involved in my talk by using them in skits or demonstrations.

For instance, I will invite a man and a woman up from the audience to perform what I call "A Day in the Life of a Russian Family." "You are the boss because you are the man," I tell him. "In Russia, it doesn't matter if your are smart or stupid, if you have a lot of money or just a single kopeck, women will respect you for the simple reason that you are a man and you are in a male dominated society."

As I'm saying this, the women usually get a little upset. I think it's okay to get people a little upset, particularly at the beginning of your presentation. Then when your talk eventually lifts them from irritation to joy, it will be even more impressive.

I always ask my participants if they want to pretend to be a Russian man or woman and usually they say, "Sure, but what are you going to do to us?"

"I'm not going to do anything to you," I say. "Just tell me if you have medical insurance." Medical insurance is an alien concept in Russia, but it is guaranteed to bring nervous laughter to American audiences.

Our day in the life of a Russian family begins at 6:00 a.m. with the woman getting up to fix breakfast. "Not just cereal," I warn my Russian woman. "You have to fry potatoes and prepare tea." Meanwhile, our Russian man gets to call out "Hurry up! Breakfast, breakfast!"

People laugh at this and the other little details of getting to work and buying food, and gradually they realize I am giving them information, but using a different approach to Soviet life than to lecture them with facts and figures. By the time this five-minute demonstration is over, everyone is certain of two things. They are glad that this poor woman, who had to go through the obstacles of Russian life, can come back to America. And they can see that I am not just going to tell them about the Soviet Union. I am going to take them there. That is how I present information in an entertaining manner.

Persuade

The third goal of public speaking is to persuade people to buy something. For speakers who are just starting out, this means convincing people that you should get another invitation to speak. You are trying to sell yourself, and to do that successfully means working toward the first two goals. You need to have something interesting to say -- information -- and you need to present it in a way that is interesting to your audience -- entertainment.

When I started speaking to groups, I thought I had to act intelligent so I would be considered an expert and get more opportunities to speak. It didn't take long to discover that the highest compliment an American can give a speaker like me is not to say that I'm very intelligent. It's to say I'm a very funny guy.

Being funny got me more speaking engagements; being intelligent helped me use those engagements to explain about life in another country. Being both funny and intelligent was the best way I found to sell myself.

While you are persuading a group of people that you have something interesting to say in an interesting way, you may want to sell something else as well. You can encourage people to visit another country, write to their Congressman, or do what I did and sell your own book.

Publishing was very tightly controlled in the Soviet Union when I lived there. The Communist Party may not be in a position to ban books any more, but a shortage of paper has much the same effect these days. When I came to the United States, I discovered the big publishing houses can make you wait almost as long as a Russian bureaucrat to get a book in print, especially if you kill fewer than ten people in your manuscript. But I also discovered you can print your own books in this country, so I wrote about my attempts to move to America and my first experiences here. Then I paid to have them printed inexpensively and sold them after my presentations.

To sell my books -- this is my fourth one -- I tell people they can learn more about Russian life by purchasing my book after my talk. "Do you want to find out what Russian women do at night and why Russian men go bald," I ask. Or I say that if my thick accent kept them from understanding something, they can read it in English in my book. That way my book becomes an extension of my presentation, a way for people to dig deeper into Russian life. If I've caught their attention, hopefully they will want to know more.

People like it when you sign your book for them. While I'm doing this after my presentation, I tell them I'm taking a big chance by ignoring the first instructions my mother-in-law gave to me for surviving in America: *<u>Don't sign anything!</u>*

People even like it when you say your book is terrible -- as long as you say it in a funny way. That shows you can laugh at yourself. It's easy to make jokes at the expense of the poor Russian people or the stupid Russian government; they are easy targets. But the speakers who have a sense of humor about themselves already have taken a big step toward achieving the goals of public speaking.

I never felt I could speak in Shakespearean English, but that's never stopped me from communicating with Americans and I was surprised that they could understand me pretty well. My primitive English has its advantages. During my lecture, people hear things in my speech that I never said. They say, "This is a great idea you have."

> **Suggestions that I like to give to immigrants on American customs: "Don't feel ashamed of your English. Many Americans have trouble speaking it properly themselves. And never refuse anything. Americans offer gifts only once, so modesty is a mistake."**

Chapter 3

How Many Bullets For a Joke?

(Using Humor In Presentations)

People like my personality, but when I started speaking to audiences I wondered if they liked my presentations. I said the same thing to every group and the people were very polite, but something was missing.

It is important to remember that if people have taken the time to come hear you speak, they want you to succeed. In fact, they will do everything they can to help you make a successful presentation.

My problem was that I didn't know how to meet the audience halfway. After one of my talks, a state senator approached me and said, "Your presentation is not too bad, but you need to add a couple of jokes."

I was floored! Here was a leader of the state, a serious and powerful person, telling me about humor. But I talked to other people and learned that in the United States, a speaker is expected to begin with a joke or two to catch the audience's attention and make them your friends. So I began to think about jokes.

Jokes

Many of the funny stories I knew from Russia were not appropriate for American audiences. My wife rejected any humor that fell into the "dumb blond" catagory. "Only other women can tell jokes about women and get away with it," she warned me. The best ethnic jokes tend to deal with Georgians, Jews and Armenians. I knew plenty of Jewish jokes, and since I'm Jewish I thought they would be fair game, but my wife also crossed them out as racist.

When you are struggling with a new language and have to think up funny things to say, it pays to keep them as simple as possible. At first, I tried words that seem guaranteed to get a laugh. Words like 'lawyer.'

> "Gorbachev is a smart guy, but I don't believe him," I tell people. "Remember, he's a lawyer. You can tell when he's lying -- his lips are moving."

I also found that any line with the word 'vodka' in it would get a laugh, expecially when pronounced with a Russian accent. "Wod-ka" was even funnier when combined in a joke, like the one I used to illustrate what happened when Gorbachev created a shortage of vodka to try to reduce drunkenness and improve productivity.

> "People had to stand in line to buy vodka and the price kept rising higher. One man who had been standing in line all day got so depressed that he announced he was going to go kill Gorbachev. He disappeared for a couple of hours, and when he returned several people asked him what happened. 'The line at the Kremlin to kill Gorbachev is even longer than the line to buy vodka,' he explained."

I gradually added other funny lines and stories to my presentations, looking for ones that illustrated the points I wanted the audience to remember from my talks. Once I knew what to look for, I never lacked for humorous material.

The Russian people are known for their sense of humor. It helps them deal with winters that last six months, bureaucrats that control their lives, endless lines to stand in, and stores with empty shelves. In Russia, humor is a serious business -- a survival mechanism for your sanity, and not just a routine at some comedy club.

> In America, if you ask "How much does a comedian get?" you might get an answer of five or ten thousand dollars. Had you asked the same question a couple of years ago in the Soviet Union, the answer might have been five or ten years in a labor camp.

In 1986, the Soviet newspaper "Pravda" wrote that jokes about the Soviet government and other jokes anti-Soviet in character were created by experts in a special department of the CIA and spread through the USSR over the Voice of America and by special agents. Pravda was often good for a few laughs, and the effect of its humor was only strengthened by the fact that it was trying to be completely serious.

Even during the darkest days of the Stalin and Brezhnev regimes, Russians were poking fun at their country. But only within the confines of the family circle, with the windows tightly closed, a pillow over the telephone, and only in the bathroom with the water running full blast. In summer there were always fewer jokes because the water was habitually turned off for a couple of months for repair work on pipes and pumping stations.

> President Reagan's favorite Russian joke: "A man paid 15,000 rubles to buy a car. He was told he would have to wait in line five years to get it. The man reluctantly agreed and put his name down for delivery on a date five years hence. 'Just be sure you deliver it in the afternoon,' he said. 'The plumber is coming that morning.'"

Funny Stories

Americans don't understand how many hours Russians spend standing in lines. Perhaps that is because when they visit the Soviet Union, Americans are not subject to the same rules of supply and demand as those who live there.

This is one of the reasons I have longed to become an American since I was nine years old. One Sunday afternoon our whole family rode the subway to one of downtown Moscow's finer restaurants. Such special occasions occurred only once or twice a year, so I was unusually excited and extraordinarily happy.

Enveloped by the noise of the subway, I imagined what we would find at our destination. Of course there would be a long line and a sign on the door warning "No Free Places". But my father would approach the distinguished doorman in a dark blue uniform and whisper something in his ear. Then we would pass into the restaurant to the dismay and wrath of the entire line.

As we walked from Sovietsky Square, I spied the line and the doorman at his post. However, on this bright Sunday afternoon my father's whisperings and even a ten-ruble tip had no influence. The doorman shrugged his shoulders and said, "What can I do? We are serving American tourists today."

The next day at school we wrote an essay that would be read by the district supervisor as an example of our accomplishments. In answer to the question "What Would You Like to be When You Grow Up?", I unburdened myself about my disappointing experience at the restaurant and concluded that I would like to be an American. An unbelievable scandal ensued, and for several years after our school was known not as Number 279, but as the school for American tourists.

I like to use humorous stories like this to make the main points in my presentations. It gives a taste of life in the Soviet Union.

Today, shortages are still a part of daily life in Russia, but as the political system changes and words like glasnost and perestroika invade the language, I find that jokes adapt to the new vocabulary. With a subject as huge, mysterious and volatile as Russia, I will never lack for jokes and funny stories that reveal a truth about the land of my birth in a memorable way:

> "A man walks into a store and, seeing the rows of empty shelves, begins to curse Gorbachev's reforms. A man in a black leather coat, trappings of the KGB known to every Soviet, walks up behind him and says, 'You are very lucky. Under Gorbachev, you may express your indignation out loud. In former times you would have been executed for anti-Soviet propaganda.' The shopper runs out into the street and yells, 'Comrades, we're in real trouble now! They don't even have enough bullets to shoot us.'"

Whenever I can't think of anything else to talk about, I tell stories about a subject that everyone can relate to and that is very close to every Russians' heart: Food. Private enterprise has yet to bring the well-stocked supermarkets of America to Russia.

> **Moscow's newest supermarket only hired two people. One to stand at the entrance and say "Nothing to buy," and the other to stand at the exit and say "Now do you believe us?"**

I had a friend in Moscow, an enterprising girl named Tanya, who once heard at work that smoked sausage was available at a small store across town. Good smoked sausage is a rare and coveted item in Moscow, and Tanya worked out an elaborate plan to get some.

Tanya knew a woman who worked at a cosmetics factory who had a friend who worked at a liquor store, whose wife was redecorating her kitchen. She also had a friend of a friend who was a butcher who liked beer. Now, the cosmetics factory, the liquor store and the butcher shop were located in three widely separated parts of Moscow. Tanya knew for the complex logistics and distances of this operation she needed a car. That's where I came in.

First stop was the cosmetics factory where we picked up the buxom, heavily perfumed middle-aged lady with numerous purses, shopping bags and all the connections. We then drove around to the back gate where two cases of kitchen tiles miraculously appeared and where dropped with a heavy thump into my trunk. Then it was a 30-minute drive to the liquor store where we deposited the tiles and picked up six cases of prime Czech beer. Twenty minutes away at our next stop we traded four cases of beer for a large quantity of smoked sausage wrapped in greasy newspaper that was clandestinely passed directly through the back door into my trunk. I assume there was much negotiating as to how much beer umptine kilos of sausage was worth because we sat awaiting the conclusion of the transaction for an incredible length of time. We ended up with two remaining cases of beer which had to go under Tanya's legs to make room for the salami.

After spending five hours and a full tank of gas, we arrived home with a car smelling of sausage and "Moscow Nights" perfume and one case of Czech beer for our pains. Tanya had her sausage and was very pleased with herself. I never did figure out where the kitchen tiles came from.

Chapter 4

Don't Be Surprised

(Memorizing The Speech)

If English is not your native tongue, preparing a presentation can be a problem. You want to use melodious sounding phrases, but they are difficult to memorize and their meaning is not always clear.

Memorizing

For my first few speeches, I tried to write my presentation and memorize it using several different approaches. I tried repeating it so many times my daughter started to cry. What's worse, by the time she was two-and-a-half she was correcting my English. It can be embarassing to be set straight by a little kid who knows more about the English language than you do.

So I tried another approach. I asked my wife to read a presentation into a tape recorder for me to repeat and memorize. Unfortunately, I started to pick up the intonation in a woman's voice. People wondered why the tone of my voice would change when I got to the parts of my speech that my wife had recorded for me. I was trying so hard to say the right words that they came out sounding like my wife.

I tried another method when I was invited to give a presentation for Law Day, a holiday in early May honoring new American citizens. This was supposed to be a three- or four-minute speech, but I worked on it for two weeks. I would jog around our neighborhood, memorizing my brief address while I stayed in shape.

A few days before my presentation I asked a friend to listen to me practice my speech. It didn't take long for me to start jogging in place -- it was the only way I could remember my presentation! Since jogging during my talk was not a practical solution, it was good that I figured that out before my presentation.

I managed to memorize it again, but the effect was rather mechanical, since I was repeating my speech word-for-word from what I had written. For a short speech, memorizing every word is not a bad idea. It can help you make the best use of your speaking time. Just be sure you practice it long enough so the words flow from your heart and not just drop from your mouth.

A Brief Example

My Law Day speech is an example of the elements that make up a good short speech -- a simple organization, touches of humor, and a message that touches people's emotions:

"I came to the United States less than four years ago. Many dramatic events have changed our world since then. The Berlin Wall tumbled down, we won the war in the Persian Gulf and the Honorable Sheri Barnard became a Mayor of Spokane.

"Just one month ago I was waiting, like you today, to receive my certificate of naturalization. I was so excited and nervous that I don't remember much about the ceremony. But I do remember that the speaker did not have a Russian accent. I'm proud and happy that the United States allowed me to become a citizen of this great and beautiful country.

"Some people say that America is a dangerous place to live. Some say that Americans are a naive and spoiled people. If it is so, why do so many countries look to America for help in time of need? If it is so, why do so many people dream of coming to this country?

"They say that America is a land of abundance, and I know it is true. America has given me every thing: a beautiful wife, a baby with blue eyes and, most important, the feeling that I am at last a free human being. As all new immigrants in this country, I was at first confused by the great variety and endless choices. In Russia I had only to choose between green cabbage and purple cabbage. Here the choices are much more complex. Like on April 15 I had to choose between 1040 long, 1040 short and 1040 EZ.

"America is a land of freedom. Some people ask me if I would like to return to the Soviet Union since now there are some freedoms there. Yes, Russian people now have freedom of demonstration, but I won't return until they also have freedom after demonstration. Besides, I am already spoiled by American life and American bureaucrats who smile even when they say no.

"America is a land of opportunity. Here we can accomplish anything we set our minds to.

"Our country is one nation under God. President Lincoln once said: A house divided against it self cannot stand. So let us work together to make this nation even stronger. And when new immigrants come to our shores they will look about them in wonder and say: WHAT A COUNTRY!"

Mini Speeches And Main Points

For longer presentations, I hit upon a system that worked much better than simply memorizing pages of words. I divided my talk into different subjects, like the shortage of food in Russia or how it is dealing with AIDS. Then I built up about five minutes of material around a good story that illustrated that subject. By adding a few jokes and comparisons with the United States, I created a mini-speech on that topic. By stringing these mini-speeches together, I could give a presentation to fit the amount of time I had to speak and the areas of greatest interest to my audience.

I build these parts of my presentation around stories because it is easier for me to remember a good story -- and the same holds true for the people who are listening to me. And if they remember the stories, they will leave my talk knowing the main points I wanted to make.

As you plan your presentation for a particular group, don't forget that your audience needs all of the help you can give to remember your main points. After you have broken the ice with your opening story or activity, state the main messages you will emphasize and give a brief overview of what your talk will be about. Then as you work your way through your stories, don't hesitate to repeat the most important points and emphasize them in unusual ways.

After the coup attempt in 1991, the Communist Party was effectively dismantled. To illustrate what a remarkable change this was, I hold up a copy of "Pravda," the party's own newspaper, from just before the coup. Then I compare it with a copy of Pravda from just after the coup. Even though most of the people I speak to can't read Russian, they have no trouble seeing that the Communist Party seal has disappeared from the paper's masthead.

Dramatic Endings

Whether you are speaking for two minutes or two hours, always end with a bang. Save your most dramatic story for the close of your presentation. We all remember movies or books with surprise endings. You want your audience to remember you as well, not just because you informed and entertained them, but because you surprised them. Just when people think that you have run out of material, I like to start a new story. That's why I always save the best ones for the end.

> An American spy has come to the KGB to give himself up. He goes into the reception room and says, "I am an American spy," but they interrupt him and, because he is a spy from an imperialist country, send him to the third floor, room 316. In room 316, the American spy informs them that he parachuted into the USSR, so they sent him to the fifth floor, department of technical applications. There they discover he is a saboteur, specializing in bridge demolition and send him to the second floor where the department of sabotage is located. After three hours of walking around the building, he hears over a loudspeaker: "Would the American spy please report to the personnel office on the first floor." There, sitting in a large office, he finds a familiar face, but now without glasses. He asks him threateningly, "What are you doing wandering around the building like you have nothing to do? The spy tries to explain that he was sent to the USSR to work, but the stern personnel director interrupts him. "If you were sent to work, get to it. We don't tolerate loafers in the country of Soviets."

Chapter 5

Who Discovered America?

(Practice Makes Perfect)

Giving a speech or making a presentation is like any other challenging activity. If you want to do it right, you have to practice.

Three years after arriving in the United States, I embarked on the path to American citizenship by memorizing a special book full of information for aspiring citizens-to-be. Then I decided to impress my wife with my new knowledge. "I know who discovered America," I announced. "It was Christopher Columbus on a Ford Pinto."

She encouraged me to keep practicing for my citizenship test, and I quickly straightened out Columbus. He came on a ship called the Pinta, not a Pinto. I practiced matching important events with their dates: 1776, 1863, 1607, 1787, 1620. My wife became concerned one night when I began to talk in my sleep and the name Virginia floated out of my lips. She felt reassured when Pennsylvania and New York followed.

When the time came for me to take my citizenship test, it was a piece of cake. My practicing made the difference, and I try to prepare my presentations with the same kind of enthusiasm.

Visualize Success

I start out with a positive attitude toward my speech. I am excited about my subject and look at each presentation as a chance to share that excitement with other people. With my enthusiasm running high, I try to visualize a successful presentation. I am informative, entertaining, even surprising. No one in the audience yawns or looks at their watch the entire time I am speaking. They are so impressed when I finish my talk, that dozens of people buy my latest book and the group invites me back for another engagement.

I also remember the words of Demosthenes, an ancient Greek orator, who said that the mark of a great presentation is not that people cheer you, but that they want to march behind you. But in the United States, that means people will buy what you are selling.

Key Words

Once you've made it this far, look at the presentation you've been memorizing. Pick out simple words or symbols and use them as reminders for each of your stories or mini-speeches. Giving a presentation is like conducting a tour of an art museum, and these symbols or words are the keys that unlock the galleries so you can share what's inside with your audience.

> A Soviet theoretician is asked to explain styles of painting. "Expressionism," he says, "is painting what you feel. Impressionism is painting what you see. Socialist Realism is painting what you are told."

Key words are powerful, but be sure to use them carefully. I once visited a U.S. embassy reception in Moscow to talk to presidential candidate Gary Hart about my problems with the Soviet bureaucracy. He listened to my story and made a few jokes about Russian bureaucrats, so I tried to compliment him by calling him a joker. Unfortunately, I called him a "jerk" instead. The silence that followed was very uncomfortable, and even though my English is better now, I am still only one misplaced consonant away from acute embarassment when I speak.

Rehearsal

When you have memorized your mini-speeches and each one's key word, it's time to rehearse your presentation. Say it out loud by yourself. Try recording your talk on an audio or video tape. Invite a friend or two over to your house and try it out on them. Have one of them time you so you can expand or contract your talk to fit the timing for your public speech.

If you plan on using props, practice with them to work out any problems. Remember, they should reinforce your main points in the most effective way possible. They should be simple and clear. And they should not be the primary means for giving information to your audience. If the props you plan to use don't accomplish these goals, don't use them; they will only detract from the strength of your message.

Storytelling

In periods when I don't have a presentation, I try to keep my skills in shape by telling stories to myself, like this one I call...

International Woman's Day

In the four years that I have lived in the United States, I have not once bought my wife a present. It is not because I love her less than I did in Russia, but because the thrill is gone. Finding a present for your best girl in Moscow is a challenge and an art.

My lanky friend, Adik, called on March 7, the eve of the international holiday for women. He asked that I meet him at the entrance to the Exhibit of Economic Achievement in northern Moscow. VDNKh, as the exhibit is known to all Russians, is a sort of cross between an amusement park and the Smithsonian Institute.

"We're going in search of presents," Adik added in a muffled and mysterious voice. How could I turn down a request like that.

March 8 is the most unpleasant holiday for male Russian citizens. Tradition dictates that they must present gifts to all the women in their acquaintance. On the day before the holiday the stores are packed with panicked men clamoring for toilet water, chocolates, flowers and those articles of female attire that men are capable of selecting.

There was some comfort in the thought that if one female on your list didn't care for her gift, you could always give it to another. But under no circumstances could a woman be overlooked; such an insult would haunt you the entire year.

As I stood beneath the towering figures of the farm girl and laborer adorning the great cement entry arch of the Exhibit, I recalled a saying that Adik, then a gay bachelor, loved to repeat when we were in college: "If a man brings flowers to his wife, it means his girlfriend stood him up." I hadn't heard the saying since Adik had married the petite acrobat from the Moscow Circus on Ice.

A heavy hand grasped my shoulder. I turned to find Adik, dressed in a long black raincoat with black leather gloves. A small bucket with a child's shovel dangled from one hand.

"Well, let's suppose the bucket is to be filled with perfume at the factory where Adik's uncle works and we'll bottle it in his kitchen. But what is the shovel for?" I wondered.

"So, do you have a treasure for your wife buried beneath some tree here?" I tried to joke.

"You'd do better to keep your jokes to yourself," Adik growled at me. "This is all your fault."

Seeing my puzzlement, he explained, "Do you remember that book you gave my wife last year?"

I tried to recall the book. It was in English. I remembered that. Was there something offensive in it? My English wasn't so good then. The book, with beautiful pictures of plants, had been on my shelf too long. Tanya was taking an English class. What a marvelous gift for Women's Day! Or so I had thought.

"That book," Adik snapped on, "is all about healthful eating, and now my wife has become a vegetarian. She'll only eat whole grains and weeds. When was the last time you saw fresh vegetables in winter. As for whole grains, only my grandma remembers when you could buy those, and she's 92 years old. Tanya rides the commuter train for two hours twice a week to get fresh milk. That's what your stupid book has done. And now you have to help me steal a present."

Adik detailed the operation facing us like a military maneuver. We would stroll inconspicuously to the large agricultural pavillion on the exhibit grounds. It might be mistaken for a huge marble palace were it not for the gold-gilded shock of wheat sprouting from the peak of the roof. Inside, in cases of thick glass, apples, bunches of grapes and even sausages glistened in perfect displays. The displays were additionally protected by a low wire fence.

Against the wall, huge linen bags were filled to overflowing the samples of the Ukraine's best: golden grains. These were Adik's goal, and he eyed them carefully from across the room.

As in all public places, an old woman, a sentry of sorts, sat near the door in a green uniform. Usually these ladies dozed or knitted clothes for their grandchildren, but this one was annoyingly alert.

I meandered casually toward her, admiring the achievements of Soviet agriculture. I moaned, I stumbled, I clutched at a display case and my chest. The old lady and several of her colleagues ran to me on spry legs.

They tugged me toward a chair. "Are you in pain? What ails you? One so young and already a bad heart."

"Maybe he just needs to sober up," chimed in a younger vistor to the pavilion, a woman with flaming hair and a harsh face.

I had to run to catch up with Adik who was striding quickly along the tree-lined lane on his long legs.

"Everything okay with your present?" I asked. I tugged at the corner of a paper sticking out of the bucket. It read: "Danger -- this grain has been treated with pesticides". I showed the paper to Adik.

"It's nonsense. They put those warnings on the displays so people won't steal the stuff. I have a friend whose wife has been eating this pavilion's diet for two years. She's fine."

On the way home, I dashed into a public toilet near the exhibit. I needed to buy presents too.

As in years past, a portly woman in a dirty-white apron with a dozen pockets stood near a burlap bag full of flowers. A threadbare gray woolen overcoat covered her shoulders. Two unshaven men drank from a single glass in the corner, celebrating the holiday early. The scent of the flowers did little to disguise the disgusting odor of the place.

The flowers were expensive, very expensive. "But it's Women's Day only once a year," the saleswoman reassured me with sparkling eyes and added a few strands of grass to the bouquet for effect. She delicately pronounced for me the Japanese word that described the horticultural artistry in which she was engaged, but in Russian it sounded like cursing.

It was late at night when I finally reached home. My mother was still awake, waiting for me. To cut short her reproaches, I extended the roses across the threshhold. She started, then looked closely at the bouquet and began to laugh. The rose buds were tied to the stems with lengths of black thread.

"Never mind," my mother calmed me. "I haven't been able to buy black thread for six months. It will come in handy."

I gave her a kiss. "Happy Women's Day, Mom."

Chapter 6

Always Keep Your Mouth Wet

(Body Language)

Before your open your mouth to speak, people know some very important facts about you from the way you act. Most authors call it body language, but at the beginning of my speaking career I just called it feeling very sick. I was collapsing before every presentation. I had a fever, my mouth was dry, and I couldn't even look at the people in front of me.

My wife suggested I visit some classes and observe other speakers in action. I didn't understand what she was talking about, since Russia doesn't have classes on speaking, or anything else for that matter, that are open to the general public.

Back when I was in Russia and my wife was pregnant, I put through a call to her in the United States. My mother-in-law answered and said Susan was at a pregnancy class.

"What?" I exclaimed. "Why do you need a class to deliver a baby? My mom always said you just have to wash the floor and the baby will jump out."

When I came to America, I couldn't believe how many different classes you can take. Classes on how to play with a yo-yo. Classes on how to wind surf. Classes on sighting UFOs. Classes on how to use a cordless phone. Classes on how to be optimistic about life. Classes, classes, classes.

There are two classes of people in Russia: pessimists and optimists. Pessimists think the country will collapse in two weeks. Optimists think it will take two months.

But I saw my wife's point and signed up for a class on public speaking. On the first day, I asked the teacher how to make a presentation. He grabbed my hands and told me to keep them under my seat and just talk.

Now, I was pretty upset, because as a Russian Jew I don't know how to talk without moving my hands. Maybe it was good advise for other people, but I had enough problems speaking English without tying my hands behind my back.

A Russian Jew walking in Moscow was carrying two big watermellons in front of his chest. A Russian farmer stopped him and asked for directions to the Kremlin. The Jew said, "Hold my watermellons." After handing the watermellons to the farmer, the Jew spread his arms wide and said, "I don't know."

Calm Your Nerves

Here are some suggestions for conquering stage fright that have been helpful for me. Before you leave for the presentation, spend a few minutes looking in a mirror. Make silly faces to get your face muscles stretched out.

Whenever I do this, I remember preparing for my first public appearance. I was looking in the mirror and saw my wife sneaking up behind me holding a mask with a big red nose and drooping mustache.

"This is for the beginning of your lecture," she said. "You will sit with the mask on and your back to the audience. I will say, 'Many Americans believe that Russians are just the same as us...'"

After I protested, she warned, "You don't know a single American joke. If you can't amuse the audience, they won't listen to you and you'll be booed out of the auditorium." The last words she pronounced with such an evil tone that I truly understood that if I wasn't funny, something awful would happen. My defense was broken, and she put the mask on me. My daughter, watching from her highchair, broke into loud wails.

Before you face an audience, try breathing deeply to calm down those pre-presentation nerves. Sometimes I have so much energy before a talk that I have to go jog in place to work it out of my system. Usually you can get your blood flowing by shaking your hands, rubbing your shoulders or scratching your head.

Warm Up Your Voice

Don't forget to warm up your voice as well. Yawn, hum a favorite song, or sing "Do, Re, Me" from the Sound of Music. It doesn't matter too much what you do to get your voice in gear as long as you give it a little exercise before you ask it to carry you through an hour-long presentation.

Singing a song is a great way to get excited about your presentation and helps you express your emotions. The day I became an American citizen, I was riding in the car with my four-year-old daughter. "Papa," she said, "let's sing 'I'm Proud to Be an American'."

"I don't know the words," I answered. That wasn't on the citizenship test.

"Then I'll teach you. Just say the words after me."

I started hesitantly but stopped singing when I noticed a policeman pulled up next to us at the light. If you're singing in your car in Russia, you'll get pulled over for sure because its a sign you're drunk. I glanced over at the policeman, but he just smiled back.

His smile made my understand for the first time that this is my country now and I have nothing to fear. I am protected by the First Amendment, and nobody can't arrest me for sing-driving.

"Okay, Emily, let's start again!" And we sang it from the top, at the top of our lungs: "I'm proud to be an American, where at least I know I'm free..."

> **My Mother-in-law Says: "This is a free country, so you can do anything you want. Just don't get caught -- especially by the I.R.S."**

I had studied the Bill of Rights for my citizenship test, and the foresight of its authors astounded me. Only recently in the USSR have new laws been adopted on freedom of religion, freedom of the press, and freedom of assembly.

Comparisons of American and Russian history involuntarily came to mind as I read about the great American leaders -- George Washington, Thomas Jefferson, Abraham Lincoln. Men of expanded minds and benevolent spirits. Compare these to the outstanding leaders of Russian history -- Ivan the Terrible, Peter the Great, Joseph Stalin. Dictators all, who ruled by blood and terror.

> **After the attempted coup last summer, the Russian media reported that many of the soldiers didn't have bullets in there rifles. This led one Russian to say to another, "Now we are really in trouble. The shortages are so bad, the government doesn't even have enough bullets left to kill us."**

When you are ready to start your presentation, whether the topic is giving thanks or avoiding tanks, body language should not be something you have to worry about. You can take classes or look for advise in books like this, but in the end you have to find your own style. Is your presentation lively? Are you fascinated by the subject of your talk? Do you want the people in your audience to enjoy their time with you? Then let them know how you feel.

Wear A Smile...

One of the ways I use body language in my presentations is to smile. As I learned from the police officer I encountered while sing-driving, a smile puts other people at ease.

I admit this was an acquired art for me, since "smiling for success" is not a Russian concept. The greatest differences between America and Russia are not tangible, like food in the stores or cleaner streets. The most important differences to me are more subtle, and chief among them is the way people treat each other. From the customs officers at the airport in Washington, D.C. where I first entered this country to the joggers in the streets of Spokane where I live, everyone has a friendly smile and a kind word. At first I saw them greet each other on the street and couldn't understand how everyone knew each other. Only gradually did I realize they were simply being friendly.

Smiling people in the stores and on the streets paled beside my discovery that in America, even bureaucrats can be friendly. This seemed too much to believe, until I realized that they said "No" almost as often as their Soviet counterparts. You just didn't mind it as much because they were so pleasant.

> **My Mother Always Says:** "In the Soviet Union, only lunatics and American tourists smile at total strangers."

For my first few presentations, I took a lesson from the bureaucrats and tried to keep an open smile on my face while I spoke. Now after countless talks, it appears automatically. It seems to help me feel more positive about what I'm going to say, and it helps the audience feel more relaxed.

...And Clothes

Unless your are speaking at a nudist colony, you will need to wear more than just a smile. Clothes send a message to your audience too, and I don't want that message to be at odds with my smile or my words. As a rule of thumb, I dress at least as well as the people I will be addressing. I am trying to sell my subject and myself, so I also suggest observing salespersons who are successful at what they do. The way they dress usually reflects what they sell and who they are selling it to -- if you want to sell men's suits, it helps to wear one -- and that is a reasonable guide to dressing for a presentation as well.

Now that you, your body and your clothes are speaking the same language, you won't have to worry that your audience will misunderstand what you say.

> **On my first day in the United States, my wife told me we were going to have hot dogs for lunch. "There is a shortage of food in the Soviet Union," I said, "but even there we don't eat dogs!"**

Chapter 7

Don't Laugh, This Is Russia!

(Final Preparations And Beginning Your Presentation)

The leaders of Russia have always valued discipline, but after I arrived in the United States I found that, in my new country, punctuality was king. This wasn't a complete surprise as I had heard a story about three workers who met in a labor camp.

Three Soviet prisoners asked each other what crime they had committed. "I was five minutes late to my office, and they are very strict on discipline," said the first man. "I was five minutes early to my office," said the second man, "and they decided I was a spy." The third man said, "I got to my office exactly on time, and they accused me of owning an American watch."

Of course, now that I am an American, I am free to own a Japanese watch like everyone else. I also have learned an important discovery that kept my speaking career from meeting an untimely end. One day I was late for a presentation to a Rotary Club, and while I was speeding down the highway in a vain attempt to get there on time, I figured out one of the secrets of a successful public speaker: Worship your calendar.

It doesn't matter if you have one presentation a month or ten next week, keep a date book of your engagements and check with it often. The day before your presentation, put a note on your bathroom mirror or on the toilet bowl -- somewhere you can't ignore it -- with the location and time of your talk.

Arrive Early

I always give myself a gift before I make a public speech: Time. I do that by arriving for a presentation as early as I can. I go to the place I will be speaking and arrange my books, Russian newspaper, and any other props. I want to get them ready now so I won't have to think about them when I'm preparing to speak.

This is the time to ask people questions. It is amazing how much you can learn in the ten or 20 minutes before your presentation begins. When I'm invited to make a presentation, I know the people belong to some group. But how many people will be there? What are their ages and occupations? What do they want or expect from my presentation? It's very rare to find a program director who will send me this information ahead of time, so this is my chance to see what kind of public I will face.

If it is older people, I try to get as close to them as possible and speak slowly.

If it is young people, I want to be ready with simple but funny jokes about life in Russia. Are they wheat farmers who want to know more about Russian agriculture?

> **Russian farmers say: This year's harvest is much worse than last year's, but at least it's better than next year's. We have four main excuses for a terrible harvest -- winter, spring, summer and fall.**

Perhaps the topic of choice is Russian politics or cooking? I can adjust my talk to give them more stories and information about what interests them. Sometimes adding one or two minutes on the right subject can do a lot to endear you to your listeners.

Set The Stage

The time before you speak also is when you want to find any obstacles to a successful presentation. Is it too hot? This is your chance to ask someone to change the temperature in the room before the heat starts putting your audience to sleep. Is there enough light for everyone to see you? Will background noise from air conditioners or the clatter of waiters picking up dinner plates distract your listeners? Ask the program director to help you make it as favorable an environment for listening as possible.

If you plan to use any audiovisual aids, check them out before you speak. They can be a useful way to highlight your main points, as long as you remember that you are the primary source of information on your subject, not the aids. Keep them simple and clear, and practice using them at home so you can incorporate them into your presentation without interrupting its flow.

Like audiovisual aids, handouts or information sheets can draw attention to your primary messages and help people keep them in mind after you finish speaking. Just be sure to wait until the end of your presentation before you distribute any information sheets to your listeners. Otherwise, they read the handout instead of listening to you.

Microphones are a blessing and a curse for public speakers. If the audience is very large, it allows everyone in the hall to hear you speak. However, I try to avoid using one whenever possible. They are subject to problems that distract your audience -- feedback, losing power, tripping you if you try to walk around the stage.

One time I stepped to a microphone to begin my presentation and it immediately went dead. "The KGB is everywhere!" I exclaimed, and I was off to a good start in spite of technical difficulties.

Their biggest drawback is the impression of distance a microphone creates between you and your listeners, especially when it is attached to a podium.

Build Rapport

When it is time to speak, my goal is to step out from behind podiums and get as close to the people in the audience as I can. I want to help them understand life in Russia, and the closer I can get to them the more they seem to retain of what I say. Sometimes they get sprayed when I pronounce a juicy Russian word, but it's much easier to build a feeling of intimacy and rapport with a group of people if you are not hiding behind a podium or a table.

Another way to build rapport is with your eyes. I read in a book that you should pick out one person at the beginning of your presentation and speak to that person. At one of my first talks, I focused on an attractive woman and directed most of my remarks to her, adding a twinkle in my eyes for good measure. It wasn't until I finished my talk that I discovered the man sitting next to her was her husband.

After that, I made it a practice to start my presentation by looking at one person, but after five or ten minutes when I feel more comfortable I shift to addressing a small group of people. By the end of my presentation, I can speak to the entire group or pick out any individual in it to focus on.

Throughout your talk, it is important to keep looking at individuals to measure their reaction to you. My presentation is divided into several parts -- mini-speeches -- and if one part is going too long and boring the audience, that is when I add some jokes or move on to the next subject.

Just a word about applause. Back in the Soviet Union, the bureaucrats designated people to applaud, shout "Hurrah, hurrah" or say that the speech is great. Normally when a big Russian leader would give a presentation, his people would be scattered around the audience to lead the clapping. A couple times when I watched Brezhnev, he changed his speech and people didn't know when to react. So he would say, "You can laugh" or "Now you can applaude." If he didn't get enough noise from the crowd, their was always recorded applause that the soundmen could play over the speakers.

Applause is nice, but most American audiences don't offer it until you are finished speaking. The exception to this is if you are speaking to a political rally or if you are the President addressing Congress. Then your audience will repeatedly interrupt you, which may explain why people have such a low opinion of Congress.

Be prepared for tough questions instead of applause when you finish. If you don't know the answer, don't be shy. Tell the best joke you can, even if it doesn't answer the question, and everyone will applaud.

At a Communist Party meeting, after an uplifting speech by the party secretary, comrade Ivanov asked: "If everything is so good, why is everything so bad?" At the next Party meeting, after a similar speech, another comrade raised his hand and asked: "If everything is so good, where is comrade Ivanov?"

The First Five Minutes

I prefer to use the first few minutes of my presentation to let the members of the audience know what they can expect during the rest of my talk -- a lively mix of funny stories, interesting facts, audience participation and jokes that get at the truth of life in a country half a world away.

The best way that I've found is to start out with a joke and then move into what I call a "Five-Minute Performance." This lets the people know what to expect and gives me a chance to work out any nervousness I'm feeling. You can tell when I'm nervous because my arms shake. This can make it very difficult to take a drink from the glass of water I like to have with me when I speak, so I recommend a brief performance to get your presentation up and running.

Typically I invite a man to come up and join me. I introduce myself to him and say "Now you are my friend. Try to imagine yourself in Russia."

He usually is laughing by now. "Don't laugh," I say. "You don't understand. If you are in Russia, you are not supposed to laugh."

To put him in the right frame of mind, I grab a large, black Russian hat -- the kind with the flaps that hang down over his ears -- and put it on his head. Now the people start to laugh, and I figure I've scored five points in the "Public Speaking" video game.

Then I joke a bit about what Russians do for pleasure. The only thing Americans know that Russians do is drink vodka. The people laugh again when I say "wod-ka" and I have an additional 20 seconds to calm my nerves and feel more confident. Only my left hand is still shaking, so I feel much better.

> **There are only three types of cocktails in Russia. One glass of vodka, two glasses of vodka, and a bottle of vodka.**

Now my performance calls for me to grab this guy's shoulders, ask him to do the same to me, and start shaking him. The audience doesn't understand, but they have a feeling it will be really funny.

I say, "We've just had a couple glasses of vodka and now we're drunk. Alcohol helps us forget about our problems, that's why it plays such a big role in Russian life."

> **One Russian to another in a bar: "Do you know the difference between a nuclear bomb and a neutron bomb? If the Americans drop a nuclear bomb on us, there will be no buildings, no beer, and no people. But if a neutron bomb hit here, there would be no people, but enough beer for everyone!"**

"You know what Americans talk about when they are drunk?" I ask the people watching us. "Sex, sports, and money. In Russia, they talk about only one thing."

Then I ask my drinking partner to repeat after me, "Do you respect me or don't you respect me?" All of this time we are shaking each other by the shoulders. The sight of two men acting like drunk Russians is not what people expect from a lecture.

> **Russian Saying: "Between socialism and communism lies the stage of social development known as alcoholism."**

The Explanation

Now comes the explanation. "Why do Russian people talk about respect? Because they were serfs for many generations. Then Stalin built forced labor camps for anyone who disagreed with him. If your government doesn't respect you, you need it from each other."

> Under Stalin, the Soviet Union was divided into three groups -- people who are going to a labor camp, people who are in a labor camp, and people who just returned from a labor camp.

The Results

My performance has lasted less than five minutes, but I've accomplished some very important things. I've warmed up my audience by getting them to laugh. I've explained a difficult concept like a Russian's need for respect in an entertaining fashion. I've given the people a taste of what to expect from the rest of my presentation.

Turning the start of your talk into a performance has another advantage. The program directors who invite people to speak at colleges, clubs or churches are looking for a "catch," something memorable about a presentation. At first I didn't understand why anyone would need a catch when the Soviet Union is so exciting. Then a doctor told me about another speaker he had heard, a woman doctor who gave a lecture on sex with a boa constrictor wrapped around her. It dawned on me that their didn't need to be any connection between a boa constrictor and a doctor talking about sex. Like a good joke or my five-minute performance, you just need a catch for people to remember you.

My "catch" has one other benefit. It warms me up to my topic and to the audience so my arms don't shake any more. Now I can take a drink of water and launch into my next story.

Chapter 8

Fool Them All By Refusing To Shut Up!

(Timing, Breaks And Questions)

When delivering a presentation, as in any aspect of life, timing and lucky breaks are essential. Consider the abortive coup last summer in Moscow. Its leaders didn't take the time to get the military firmly behind them. They didn't arrest Boris Yeltsin or cut his phone lines, which was a lucky break for him. The coup leaders didn't get any breaks from the international community. And when their plans came unraveled, they didn't have enough time to fly out of the country. As a result, now they are doing time.

> Former Soviet Defense Minister Yazov, one of the plotters of the failed coup, should have taken his own advice. When asked several years ago about the possibility of a military coup, he replied that it was not possible. The Ministry of Defense was divided into so many departments with so many bureaucrats, he said, that they could never reach a consensus on when to start a coup.

The Beginning

Let's consider timing. Suppose you want to make a good impression on your audience when you are going to make a speech. Do you launch into your subject ten minutes early and embarass everyone who walks through the door by stopping in mid-sentence and staring at them? Probably not, at least if you want to win friends, influence people and get invited back.

As I've discovered, Americans like events to start on time, so be sure to give your presentation a timely beginning. Listeners pay close attention at the start of any talk. They are curious about you and what you have to say. Whether you start with a five-minute performance or just a joke, remember to let them know the main points of your presentation and give them a feel for what your speech will be like.

Why And When To Break

If you are speaking for an hour or less, your audience can probably get by without taking a break. If your presentation lasts more than 90 minutes, plan on having at least one and possibly several short breaks. Of course, take your audience members' special needs into account when figuring when and if to give them a break. Kids can't listen as long as adults. I suggest a shorter talk rather than breaks for them, since gathering them back together may take all of the rest of your speaking time.

In Russia, breaks are a way of life. Some workers spend more time on breaks than they do at work.

For years, Russians have only pretended to work. This was because the government only pretended to pay them.

Russians use their breaks to stand in line for food or run the endless errands imposed by a society suffering from shortages of everything.

A Russian factory recently tried to break the break habit and inject some Western-style punctuality into its workforce, but it only served as a reminder of how intrenched breaks are in Russian life.

"Because we are moving to a free market economy," said the Russian factory newspaper, "we must work more productively. This means workers will no longer have breaks for lunch, for smoking, to go to the bathroom, to go to movie theaters, to play soccer, to celebrate weddings..."

In America, successful public speakers want to give their listeners a break, and for very selfish reasons. Your audience is most attentive when you begin your talk, but after a while their concentration inevitably slips. Letting them know you will give them a break in five minutes allows them to concentrate again on what you are saying, so your message reaches a more receptive audience. Then when they have had a chance to stretch and find a restroom, you begin the next part of your talk with attentive listeners instead of a room full of extras from "Night of the Zombies."

The End

Not only do breaks keep listeners more attentive, studies show the people in your audience recall more of what you say just before and after a break. The other time their memory is sharpest is when the speaker says, "And in conclusion..." That's why speakers like to end by emphasizing their most important messages; it's what listeners keep on the tip of their brains at the end of a presentation.

Speaking of the end, be sure to finish on time. This is just as important as starting on time, since groups like business people or college students often get up and leave when a speaker talks too long. Better to leave them wishing for more than to tell them everything and leave them wishing you hadn't. Unless of course you are a lunatic and an egotist like I am. Then continue to talk, but people may not believe what you say.

> Gorbachev visited the Baltic republics and spoke to the people through a local interpreter. After speaking for several minutes, the translator only said one sentence. Several more minutes of Gorbachev's talk, and again only one sentence. When Gorbachev finished, the translator spoke a slightly longer sentence. Gorbachev asked his own interpreter what the local interpreter had said. "He said 'Gorbachev is lying' whenever you paused, and when you finished he added 'He just finished lying.'"

Handling Questions

Back in Moscow in 1985 when I was working for CBS News, I remember reading my first article about Acquired Immune Deficiency Syndrome. AIDS was described in the government-controlled paper as an American malady that had been created by the C.I.A. and the Pentagon.

The American media has returned the compliment since then with stories of AIDS cases in Russian jails and the lack of disposable needles in Russian hospitals. The disease has been in the news a lot and many of the people in my audiences know these facts, so I prefer to deal with touchy subjects like this by telling a story. In this case, it's about an experience I had a few days before I emigrated from the Soviet Union.

After my nine-year struggle with the Soviet authorities to emigrate, their permission caught me unprepared. I went to the U.S. embassy -- I took to calling it "my" American embassy -- and was told, "It's nice that the authorities will allow you to leave, but first you need to have a blood test to determine if you have AIDS."

I asked how I could check my blood, and they gave me the address of a small laboratory on the other side of the city that was open a couple days a week and only a few hours at a time. When I arrived there, I found a line of 500 people, which isn't too bad when you consider that there were only two or three labs in the entire Soviet Union qualified to perform this test. I joined the line and waited my turn.

> One Russian asked another man in line, "Is it a long wait?" "I couldn't say," said the second man, "I'm new here myself. I've only been waiting two months."

Most lines in the Soviet Union are unruly, particularly if people are waiting to get food and someone warns them there are only enough potatoes for everyone to have two. Then they charge forward in a mad scramble to grab the precious spuds. But this was an AIDS laboratory with enough AIDS for everyone, so the line was very calm.

I hadn't brought anything to read to pass the time, not having expected such a long wait, so I struck up a conversation with an older woman next to me who looked like she would like to talk. I asked her why she was standing in the line, since I had read about AIDS as a disease that struck mostly young, sexually aggressive people. Russian women in their 50s were not in the market for sex, at least from what I could tell.

"I'm standing in line because I want to check my blood for AIDS," she assured me. Besides, she added, there are a lot of nice people in this line and she could talk as much as she wanted with them. "No one in my family wants to listen to me."

"But why do you think you have this disease," I persisted. In reply, she pointed to a sign on the outside wall of the laboratory that listed the main symptoms of AIDS. The symptoms were listed in the form of questions, and the first one read: "Do you feel tired?"

"That's how I feel," she declared, "so it must be AIDS."

Of course there were only a few cases of AIDS in the entire Soviet Union at that time, so it probably wasn't to blame for the fact that most of the Russian people felt tired most of the time.

> **Timely Logic:** Average Russians believe Japan and Russia will not have too many cases of AIDS. "It's a disease of the twentieth century," they say, "but Japan already is in the twenty-first century, while Russia is still in the nineteenth."

The next symptom on the list was what worried me: "Do you have contact with foreign tourists?" My wife is an American, but I was smart enough to keep my mouth shut so nobody in the line found out.

Encourage Your Listeners

Questions about deadly diseases aren't the only ones that can raise your blood pressure. Consider the strange questions public speakers often have to answer when they finish their presentations and ask the audience for its response. Or, what's worse, when someone asks for questions at the end of a talk and gets only silence.

Early in my speaking career I discovered how to encourage hesitant audiences to voice their questions and turn a one-way flow of information into a two-way discussion. I bring my presentation to an obvious end, ask for any questions, and then fool them all by refusing to shut up. I tell a few jokes or brief anecdotes, leaving about two seconds of silence between jokes for anyone with a question to raise their hand or speak out.

This way my listeners have a minute or two to think about what I've been saying and decide if they want more information about something in my speech. I get a chance to tell jokes or stories that I didn't have time to use in my main speech. I think of the answers I give to questions as a continuation of my talk. Any questions?

Chapter 9

The Russians Are Coming!

(Research)

"Nyet! I can't agree. It's too hot in California for people from Belarus."

Nyet -- no -- is the most widely used word in the Russian language. But you don't have to travel half way around the world to hear it. Just come to the Refugee Multi-Service Center in Spokane, Washington. It's in the Employment Security building where I spend several hours each week.

The walls at the Refugee Center are formed with free-standing dividers, and at any time it is possible to hear a half dozen conversations in as many languages. The area around my desk is frequently transformed into a Russian club, and according to Russian tradition our differences of opinion are backed up not by solid arguments, but only by loud voices and an unending stream of nyet, nyet, nyet.

Observe

To prepare a great presentation, you have to more than go to the library to read *Spy* magazine or watch political humorist Mark Russell on public television. I rely more on my contact with immigrants to keep up to date on events and attitudes in our homeland. The technical term for this activity is "research," and no matter what topic you speak on, research is essential. I find it very rewarding to observe these new arrivals as they discover American culture, but I also enjoy helping them adjust to their new life and easing their encounters with American bureaucracy. So I am doubly pleased to report that, at least as far as my new hometown is concerned, the Russians are coming.

Listen

Listening to the immigrants, you might conclude that rumors abound in both Russia and America about the promised land called Spokane. The secret is out, and Russian immigrants who have lived a few months in other parts of the country are saving their kopecks and pennies to buy a car that will get them to Spokane. They are coming from California, Colorado, Massachusettes, Idaho and even Seattle. Several emigres living in New Jersey rented a U-Haul to transport, not their furniture, but their family members to Spokane.

Every week brings more immigrants. In February of 1991 there were less than 150 Soviet emigres in Spokane county. By the end of the year there were over 600. And more are on the way. With the changes now occurring in the former USSR -- the break-up of the union, the impending famine, liberalized emigration policies -- it is hard to predict just how many people will choose to start a new life abroad.

It seems like only yesterday that I emigrated from Russia, but the calendar tells me that four years have passed since Soviet President Mikhail Gorbachev "exiled" me to Spokane.

Life as an emigre has been easy for me compared to other refugees, for I have an American wife who helped unlock the mysteries of my new country. Immediately upon my arrival she presented me with a list of my responsibilites as an American husband: work, support the family, help around the house and 53 other minor points. As a Soviet man, it took some time to accustom myself to some of them: kiss my wife on the cheek and say "Good-bye, Honey!" when I leave for work, buy insurance, think... When I asked about my rights at home, I was told curtly, "You have the right to remain silent."

Get Involved

Now I am trying to help my former countrymen through the difficult adaptation to a free life in America. In the process, I find a steady stream of examples to use in my presentations.

Not long ago I accompanied a recently arrived immigrant to the store. She paid the cashier for the items in her cart except a toothbrush, which she stuck in her pocket. When I told her she must pay for the toothbrush, she pointed to a large cardboard display of brushes which proclaimed in large letters "Buy One, Get The Second Free". "I only want the second one," she explained.

One day I was visited by a Russian immigrant who had travelled around the US for nearly a year looking for a good place to put down roots. I showed him the US map and pointed out the advantages of various regions of the country. The man rejected California -- too many people, Florida -- too humid, Arizona -- too hot. Obviously this was one Ukrainian who had learned to steel himself against the multitude of choices he now faced in America, for at last he declared, "If those are the only fifty states you have to choose from, I guess I'll stay in Spokane."

I was first introduced to Eastern Washington's Russian emigre community, when several families of Pentacostals and Baptists arrived in August 1989. My first assignment was to help a family from the Chernobyl region to undergo medical exams.

Anna, a mother of nine children, was pregnant and I could sense that she was very uncomfortable in the doctor's office. While in the former USSR the majority of doctors and almost all gynecologists were women, Anna's new doctor was a man. But after several visits, Anna grew accustomed to the doctor and even joked with him. He once chided her for putting on too much weight, but Anna had her reply ready. "It is not my fault," she said. "In Belarus I had to walk a half mile to the lake to wash clothes, I hauled wood for the stove and worked hard. Here the church has provided us with a cozy house and a washing machine. There's nothing for me to do. Besides," she added with a wink, "we didn't have corn chips and peanut butter at home."

Early one morning the phone rang. "Uncle Matvei, Uncle Matvei!" I recognized the voice of Anna's daughter. "Mama's gone to the hospital. The baby's coming."

When I arrived breathless at the hospital, Anna was leisurely touring the birthing room. She noticed my harried state and was quick to reassure me, "Nothing will happen until after lunch." When I translated this for the doctor he asked why she had come so early. Anna explained that it was just habit. "In Belarus the roads are bad and by the time you find a sober driver... And then the tractor can break down. Well, it's just better to be early."

"How do you like the room?" I asked. Anna was impressed by the great variety of medical instruments carefully arranged along the walls and the neatly made bed in the center of the room. She noted that with her last baby, seven other women had been in the room giving birth at the same time. "It's nice to have company," she noted. "Does the bed have handles?" The nurse pointed them out. "Okay then, let's get busy."

After several hours of translating the doctor's exhortations to "push, push, push," I witnessed the arrival of the first American citizen in the Russian refugee community.

What I Learned

When the first families began coming to Spokane, I could remember the names of all the children. But this fall, I helped to register over 60 new Soviet kids in District 81 schools. Their parents also go to school to learn English. But not all. Some women are already studying to become nurses, while some of the men are working at the aluminum factory and construction sites.

The children and women adapt most rapidly to American life. During my forty years in Russia I saw only a handful of women driving cars. The law even forbids women to drive buses. But here many of the immigrant women have received driver's licenses and have added words like headlights and carburetor to their vocabularies.

Immigrants quickly master the art of consuming. Many of them deserve a black belt in shopping. If you see someone in the store trying to sniff the meat through the celophane, like my mother did when she visited me, or someone with a basket full of dry onions, beets and smoked herring, you can bet they have recently arrived from Russia.

When I ask newly arrived immigrants what plans they have for the near future they almost always answer: "I want to buy a big car, rent an apartment and find a job with a no-nonsense boss." After a few months the same question elicits slightly different answers: "I'd like a Japanese car, a house in a nice neighborhood on the South Hill, and my own business."

Chapter 10

Secret Ballots and Other Mysteries

(Speaking Of History And Current Events)

Every autumn Americans read the results of political polls, then they go to the polls to vote -- and if they live in Chicago, they often vote for Poles as well. That means if you give presentations on a subject of political interest, like Russia's experiment with democracy, you can line up plenty of speaking engagements before Election Day.

Help Them Remember

Most of my talks revolve around history and current events. Speaking to people about these topics is very rewarding, but it requires a special effort to give your listeners the background they will need to understand your topic.

For instance, when I speak to political groups, I try to explain what politics in Russia was like before Gorbachev. For instance, Soviet elections under Stalin always had a big turnout. In one election, 130 percent of the people voted. Everyone voted because they were afraid not to vote, and if they did it twice, so much the better. You have to remember Stalin killed 45 million people. People were afraid of him, they admired him, they called him "Father of the Nation," and many of them would have voted for him even if there had been another name on the ballot -- which there never was.

Under Brezhnev, the Communist Party ran elections on the principle of bribery rather than fear. They would distribute packages of food at the polling places as an enticement, and they managed to get 99.9 percent of the people to vote. Of course, voting in those days didn't take much mental effort since there was still only one name on the ballot.

> One man who went to vote received a ballot wrapped up in a package which he was supposed to put in the ballot box. When he tried to open the package, the election officials got very irate. "Are you crazy?" they asked. "What are you trying to do?" "I want to know who I'm voting for," replied the man. "You're not supposed to know who you are voting for," explained the official. "This is a secret ballot."

Tell Stories

Even under Brezhnev, the Soviet Union was so complicated that when I tried to explain it in my presentations, I couldn't advocate a simple message like "We ought to just nuke 'em." That upset some of the conservative groups that invited me to speak. They expected me to say the Soviet Union was an evil country, but when you've grown up inside it, the situation did not seem so black and white. On one hand it is an evil society, but it is also a paradise -- created by dictators.

During Brezhnev's time, many people joined the Communist Party so they would have access to food and consumer goods. Then under Gorbachev food started getting scarce. One morning, a crowd lined up to buy meat. At six o'clock, an official came out to say, "If you are not a member of the trade union, you can go home. We won't have enough for anybody else." Some of the people in line turned and left without a word.

Three hours later, the official appeared again, saying "No meat for Jews," and another group of people in the line walked away. Around noon, even the trade union members were told to leave. Finally, only Communist Party members remained in line. They waited all afternoon until about six in the evening, when the official made one last announcement.

"Unfortunately, there is not enough meat even for communists." As they shuffled off, one disappointed shopper remarked that the Jews got a better deal. "They only had to wait three hours for nothing. We had to wait all day."

> **An American dog asked a Russian dog about Gorbachev's reforms. The Russian dog said that life under Gorbachev is much better. "I can bark all I want," he said, "and my leash is now one meter long. The only problem is they moved my food two meters away."**

Give Credit Where It's Due

Gorbachev's reforms allowed people to talk about subjects that had not been open for discussion before. Nuclear energy became a hot topic after the Chernyobl nuclear plant blew up. Someone asked Gorbachev if it was safe to eat apples grown near the plant, and he replied "Certainly, just remember to bury the core very deep."

> **The best thing I can say about Gorbachev is that Stalin and Brezhnev were worse. A favorite Russian saying from a few years ago had a government official warn that Brezhnev brought the country to the edge of the abyss. "But now that Gorbachev is in power," he said, "we are taking a great leap forward."**

It may sound like I am damning the last president of the Soviet Union with faint praise, but until the August coup attempt against him, Gorbachev was still committed to the Communist Party. Now that popular revolutions have rolled across Eastern Europe and an unsuccessful coup in the Soviet Union has led to the Communist Party being outlawed in one republic after another, Russians joked that soon the only place where it will be safe to be a communist will be America.

I give Gorbachev credit for opening the country to political reforms, but some of them have not worked out so well. Take the idea of having more than one party. It is good in theory, expecially in countries like the United States where you have plenty of practice with it, but when Russia held multi-party elections the ballot was flooded with candidates.

> **Russians haven't figured out yet that a democracy is where everyone votes, not where everyone runs.**

As for Russia and the other republics going capitalist, most people have forgotten that they already have tried it under the Tsars with mixed results. One popular saying recognizes this circular flow of history.

> **Question: "What is socialism?" Answer: "The longest way from capitalism back to capitalism."**

Russian history is too complicated for Americans, so this is my way of making it understandable for my listeners.

> **Stalin, Brezhnev and Gorbachev were riding on a train when it came to the end of the rails. Stalin blamed the engineers and ordered them killed, but the train was still stopped. Brezhnev said 'Let's close the windows, rock back and forth and pretend we are still moving.' When the passengers asked Gorbachev for his solution, he said 'I won't have any solutions until I can get to a phone. Then I'll call my wife and ask her what to do.'"**

Reaching A Conclusion

After you've told them about history and current events, people inevitably ask about the future. I don't have a crystal ball, but I know enough about Russia to make some educated predictions.

For instance, when people ask me how Yeltsin fits in Russian history, I say "Perfectly!"

Shifts in Russian leadership have historically moved from the bald to the hirsute -- from the chrome-domed Lenin to the brush cut Stalin, from Khruschev to Brezhnev. Which brings us to Mikhail Gorbachev, who is nearly as bald as a darning egg, and his upstart successor Boris "blow-dried" Yeltsin.

Until Russia's leaders rein in the military, all of their other reforms will lack a sense of permanence. The temptation will be to solve the country's problems with discipline and tanks. In the long run, Russia should become a peaceful and productive member of Western civilization. But in the short run, my former country's difficulties remind me of a joke.

Georgian and an Armenian were boasting of the accomplishments of their ancient cultures. "We dug 100 meters underground and found a wire," said the Armenian. "This means that 2,000 years ago we had telephones." "Well, we dug 100 meters underground and found nothing," said the Georgian. "This means that 2,000 years ago we had radios!"

For the next few years, Russians also will have to dig deep into their resources and may not find much they can be proud of, but at least they are headed in the right direction.

At an agriculture conference in Moscow, the committee convened to report on achievements in the new countries of the Commonwealth. The delegate from Moldova stood and reported that this year they had their largest potato harvest ever and a new strain of potato had cut the growing season to just two months. Stormy applause greeted his report. The delegate from Ukraine rose and reported similar results, stating, "We were able to harvest after just six weeks." The audience stood and applauded loudly. Finally, a Chukchi, representing the people of the Far North stood and proudly reported, "We planted potatoes on May 1 and harvested on Victory Day, May 9!" Gasps went through the crowd. A delegate asked in amazement, "But, how could you do that?" The Chukchi replied, "We were very hungry."

Chapter 11

Matvei in the Lions Den

(Speaking To Different Audiences)

One day I got a call from a man who introduced himself as the program director for the Lions Club. I thought, "Lions Club? Is he working for the zoo?"

Finding The Right Places

I didn't know about the variety of clubs in this country. In Russia they have a police club, a KGB club, a movie actors club and a club for the veterans of the Great Patriotic War, but that was it. Here they have the Lions Club, Eagles Club, Rotary Club, Kiwanis Club and many more. I thought I could make a living just speaking to service clubs.

The only problem was I found most private organizations don't have enough money to pay speakers. When I was first getting requests to speak, I used to go just to tell my story -- I didn't care about the money. Then I started thinking about reimbursement. If you want to get paid, the best clubs to speak to are located downtown with all of the banks and law firms. Also look for clubs located in a good neighborhood with big houses.

There is nothing wrong with persuing a well-heeled audience, but remember speaking to a group is a lot like making friends. Most friendships are based on mutual attraction and the ability to meet each others needs. The right audience for you is the one that wants to hear what you have to say. The right audience also offers you what you want the most: visibility, applause, money, a forum to express your views, or a combination of these things.

Learn Something New

While your are at it, you may even learn something new. One of my first presentations was for Weight Watchers. This organization doesn't exist in Russia, so I was interested in visiting one of its meetings.

I remembered back in Moscow when I was working for CBS News, Diane Sawyer came to do a story about women who are struggling to improve their image. She asked me to find a club where Soviet women were losing weight. So I found a club like this, where women would come to talk about diets and how to lose weight, and I asked them for permission to have CBS film their meeting.

They said it would be great to film the women going to the scale to check their weight. Unfortunately, they had only one scale and the first woman broke it.

When I spoke to the Weight Watchers meeting in the US, I made a very general presentation about life in Russia, but as soon as I finished and asked for questions, one woman raised her hand and asked about Russian diets.

"Russian diets?" I wondered. How do I explain to this woman -- who buys special food and who writes what she eats everyday in a journal while counting her calories and cholesterol -- about a Russian diet?

"Russian diets?" I said to her. "A Russian diet is when you eat everything you can steal. Russians used to eat from four food groups: sugar, salt, mustard and horseradish. Now only horseradish is left."

I was surprised that my answer made such a good point that everybody started to laugh and applaud. This was the first time I realized I could use a joke to give a lot of knowledge in a few words. It gave me some idea of what I could do with my knowledge of Russian life and a limited ability to speak English.

Surrounded

As you can guess by now, I like to use stories to illustrate my talks. Take the Russian people, for instance. It is much more interesting to talk about the women I have known than to talk about Russian politicians that I never met.

When I lived in Russia, I was constantly surrounded by women: my mother, my sisters, teachers, doctors. And then there were the eight woman, ages 22-61, with whom I shared a tiny room, known officially as Laboratory No. 227. Until my marriage to an American, I was, at least in name, the boss of this assortment of female talent.

Our work day began in the same way every morning, except during the three summer months. By 8:10 the last of my fair employees would appear, breathless, at the doorway of our long narrow lab and squeeze between the rows of sagging tables to her place. As the women peeled off the heavy dark layers of winter's protective clothing, they exchanged the latest gossip and news. Then silence ensued and all eyes turned toward me. This was my cue to step outside while my female colleagues removed their more intimate winter garb: a variety of long-johns, leg warmers and heavy wool socks. The corridor hosted a sort of morning men's club, as all males from other offices gathered there for the duration of the disrobing ritual. Conversation centered on hockey and politics, always in that order.

When precisely thirty minutes had passed, a hand clutching an electric tea kettle appeared through our door. I filled the kettle in the bathroom, and then, donning what I assumed to be an authoritative expression, I strode boldly back into the lab. My tea cup, freshly rinsed, stood side by side with eight others, surrounding a chipped plate of yellowing sugar cubes and stale cookies. This scenario repeated itself every working morning without fail.

On a particularly frigid January morning when I reentered my lab, Olga, a young woman with a peasant face and pug nose, was telling a joke, hoping to warm her comrades with a little laughter. I believed her husband worked for the KGB, so I tried to ignore her challenging behavior.

"So, do you know why we have only one political party, the Communist Party?"

Our silence encouraged her to laugh at her own cleverness as she answered, "We're so poor that we simply couldn't afford to feed another party!"

Olga failed to hold the attention of her audience for long. All eyes turned toward Vera, our secretary, who took night classes at the chemistry institute. At the last class, while her fellow students explored the properties of polymers, Vera conducted her own brand of research. She concocted a transparent liquid, something on the order of verathane, and now she applied it gingerly to the tips of her fingers with a delicate brush.

"It's great! she exclaimed. "My polish will last five times as long now. Even through dish washing. Line up, girls, and I'll give you a sample."

The stuff smelled strongly of alcohol. In an attempt to break up this party and show them who was boss, I said in a stern voice, "Either use up all your magic glue or hide it well. If the cleaning lady finds it, she's sure to drink it."

"She will drink it!" several laughing voices echoed in agreement.

But our secretary wasn't finished demonstrating her inventions. I postponed my hopes to get some work done for another fifteen minutes. Vera mysteriously unveiled a small bottle filled with green liquid.

"Here I've cooked up some excellent shampoo. My girlfriend tried it the other night. She said her boyfriend wouldn't leave her alone. She doesn't have a hair dryer, so she stuck her head in a warm oven for 15 minutes after using my shampoo. I think that helped bring out the scent."

Most of the morning would thus pass away. Then, twenty minutes before our lunch break the women all disappeared on their daily quest for groceries and other necessities. Only Zina, a kind and matronly woman, and I remained behind. My mother was in charge of shopping at our home, and Zina's father, an old Bolshevik now ill and broken from serving too many dictators, received food packages from a special store. They fed the whole family, and Zina even brought goodies for the office from time to time. Zina and I developed a special talent for screening telephone calls, trying to guess who might be looking for my subordinates and for what reasons.

What joy there was when the women returned, often long after lunch ended, laden with purchases! Society judged women by the size of their shopping bags -- a bulging bag meant a good wife and mother. Since food and consumer goods shortages have plagued Russia for many years, the verb "to buy" lost all meaning long ago. The terms "to obtain" (always implying with great difficulty) and the more energetic "to snap up" currently denote a score in shopping parlance. More frequently than in other offices, we celebrated the bagging of tender ham from Yugoslavia or Icelandic herring in wine sauce. The women shared their triumphs in a fraternal way and their equal division stole another hour from the work day.

Natasha, one of the younger women in the office, moved slowly and deliberately. She shuffled into work one morning, with obvious signs of an impending joyful event preceding her, covering her face with her hands. But nothing could hide her bruised and swollen eye. Her second husband subscribed to simple Russian values, and when he couldn't find the words to get Natasha moving, he resorted to the old methods. The bruise soon disappeared under the practiced hands of our labs workers, who fortunately found a little foundation from Poland that did just the trick. They also advised Natasha to be very sweet to her husband and prepare him a special dinner.

Natasha took their advice to heart and appeared after lunch with a bulging and thrashing plastic bag. Natasha had scored some fresh (read: live) fish, the coveted prize of every Soviet housewife. She proudly displayed the ugly whiskered face of a huge catfish. The experienced Zina took charge and filled the plastic bag with water to keep the fish "fresh" until dinner time.

Leaving the fish to flop in its bag, we gathered in the dingy corridor for a union meeting. The topic of the meeting was complex: how to divide three "Russian Beauty" carpets among 107 employes. Opinions were split. The majority favored drawing numbers from a hat. The more politically conscious managers, however, felt the carpets should go to workers who had demonstrated the greatest productivity.

At that point, our party chief, dressed in a dark suit accented with a clutch of war medals on the left lapel, stepped forward. He hated to speak publicly, and his eyes always bugged out when he started to talk. "Com..." A chorus of screams and screeches swallowed the end of "comrades".

The crowd of frantic workers parted to reveal a whiskered monster slithering and flopping across the hardwood floor. Natasha bit her lip to stifle a scream.

"Comrades, let's not panic," barked the chief in his best commander's voice. "I never saw the likes of this at the front," he muttered under his breath. The former colonel agilely scooped up the fish and cleanly whacked its head against the floor several times.

The carpets fell into the hands of a manager, the trade union leader and an anonymous personage who didn't even work at our institute.

On pay day old crippled Sasha always showed up with two swollen briefcases. These were Sasha's portable display cases; usually they contained cosmetics and fine apparel. All goods wore colorful plastic bags with foreign brand names printed in large, bold letters. This alone inflated the price of Sasha's wares astronomically.

Once again, the women forced me into the hallway while they measured, tried on and examined these foreign delights. One day Sasha called me back with an imploring look and said, "Matvei, you've got to help me out. I only have one Czech brassiere left. I'll let you have it for practically nothing." That meant only a 130 percent mark as opposed to the usual 200 percent.

"But, Sasha, I'm not even married. What would I do with it?" And in comic answer to my own question I put the band of lace and eyelets on my head. I expected peals of laughter to reward my cleverness, but only open mouths and wide eyes gaped at me. The director of the institute, a tall skeleton of a man in thick glasses, stood over me.

Behind his back we called him the "mole." In addition to his blindness, the "mole" also spoke in a manner unique, but often unclear. Individual sounds could be readily distinguished, but somehow they never made it into understandable words. Perhaps that is how he survived under Stalin and remained director of the institute for 36 years.

The mole extended his bony finger in the direction of my head with a puzzled expression on his face. Lena, a tall girl in stockinged feet (she had just tried on a pair of French high boots), jumped forward to my rescue.

"Comrade Director, we have a pregnant worker here," Lena nodded toward Natasha, who as usual was chomping on some tasty morsel. "The doctors say she will have twins, and just in case they are Siamese twins, Matvei has found this special cap. It fits two heads at once. His friend sent it from America. They don't have much to do there and are forever coming up with such useless items."

The director nodded in agreement, but Lena couldn't stop herself. "You wouldn't believe it, but there, in the heart of rotting capitalism, they actually advertise in the newspapers to find husbands."

"Now you are lying," broke in Katya, a single girl, whom the right man had eluded for too many years. All the women jumped into the conversation, completely forgetting about me, the director, and my Czech bra.

Now I know Lena was right. One of my first surprises upon arriving in America came from this newspaper ad: "A large, kind woman (I'm working on the weight problem) desires to meet a gentleman, aged 35-50. For the right person, I am prepared to do everything."

Of course, I don't believe that this American woman could do everything. Certainly she could not prepare a fine pot of borsch from a bare beef bone and three moldy beets like the women in my lab could.

Chapter 12

Russian Life Is No Game

(Speaking To Schools)

Let me warn you, speaking to schools is a tough job. There is very little money, but I felt it was my responsibility to tell the younger generation about my country. It is tough because usually I had to speak in five or six classes in one day.

At first I just repeated the same talk to each class, but soon I was adding slides of Russia and showing things I had brought with me from there, for example a camera. But it's not enough to show what you brought; you have to tell kids why you decided to show them that item.

A Russian camera is very big and heavy. I told the classes that it was produced at a military factory, the same place they produce periscopes for submarines. "One time I dropped it from the third floor and it still works just fine," I said. "It is very primitive, with no delicate electronic parts."

"In a way it is just like Russian life," I added. "Primitive, but tough."

Another time I brought a big, sharp fork. I asked the kids to tell me why a Russian fork is big and sharp. "It's big because you want to grab as much meat as you can when there isn't much of it," I answered. "It's sharp because the meat is very tough. Sometimes you need an ax."

Play Games

I like to play games with kids during my presentation. Maybe it will help teachers to do something like this. When you are talking to fifth and sixth graders about freedom or a shortage of food, they don't understand. In the United States, if you don't have five different kinds of pizza, that's a shortage of food. When you are talking about dictatorship and say that one person can give an order and kill 45 million other people, it doesn't impress them.

So I started carrying candies with me to play a game. "If you want to understand Russia," I said, "you have to play by Russian rules." I would pick out the biggest boy in the class and say, "You are the dictator and here are your candies. The rest of the students are your people, and you have to divide these candies between your people." I warned him that there were not enough candies for everyone. "How are you going to divide them up?"

Usually I would start the game by telling the class tyrant to put two candies in his own pocket. "You are the boss. You can give yourself two candies." Then I'd ask if he had some friends. "Bring them up front to divide the candies. Give each of them two candies, then have them tell the rest of the class to stand in line for what's left."

While the kids are standing in line to buy candies, I stand behind the line saying "Not enough candies for everybody. You better storm them." Finally the kids follow my advise and jump on the leaders.

"This is Russian life," I explain. "If you want to survive, you have to fight."

Catch Their Interest

Speaking to college crowds can be as challenging as dealing with a younger group, although for different reasons. Students like to ask tricky questions, and often they don't trust anyone who was invited to speak to them by the college administrators.

I also figure many students don't know a lot about Russia, so I try to relate my stories of Russian life to subjects they can easily understand.

Does economics have them confused?

"Just think how Gorbachev felt," I tell them. "He had 100 economists working for him, but only one of them was smart. Gorbachev's only problem was that he didn't know who was the smart one."

Perhaps I have an audience full of pre-med students. I describe an examination in a Russian medical school that was too tough for one student.

A Russian pre-med student was afraid he would fail an important exam, so he warned his professor that if he gave him a failing grade, the student would stab his own heart with a knife. The professor wasn't impressed and flunked him anyway. When a second professor said he feared that the student would carry out his threat and it would be the first professor's fault, he was told not to worry. "He's such a lousy student," explained the first professor, "he'll never find his heart."

Most students are eager to learn about other cultures, especially if you can catch their interest. Get them involved, tell some stories, and you can end up with a full schedule of speaking engagements at schools and on the college circuit.

Although humor is an important part of any presentation, you can't always get by on jokes and funny stories. The following is an example of an informative talk I have given on a very serious subject -- the new Russia.

Back to the New Russia: The Waking Giant

> **Russian Proverb:** "Everything is forbidden, but nothing is impossible."

Should a miracle occur to bring Lenin, the leader of the Bolshevik Revolution, back to life, he would feel quite at home in the new Russia of 1992. Gazing about, he would see many things familiar to him in the Russia of 1917, including the blue, white and red of the tsarist tri-color flag. Many of the cities, streets and squares that were renamed in the twenties and thirties to honor revolutionaries and communists once again bear the old Russian names that Lenin knew. The ancient city of Tver has cast off its bolshevik alias "Kalinin." Leningrad, which once proudly served as a tribute to Lenin's life and work, now again honors its founder, Tsar Peter.

Lenin's arch-enemies, the Romanovs, have returned to St. Petersburg in the form of Vladimir Romanov, the nephew of the last Russian Tsar, Nikolas. Even a descendent of the old aristocratic Golitsyn family, who survived the post-revolutionary repression, has reentered the political scene. A myriad of political parties, bearing names of a century ago, fight for political influence: socialists, democrats, anarchists, and peasant-worker parties.

Ration coupons for food and everyday necessities hark back to the econimc chaos in Russia during WWI. Lines form for bread and soap. American philanthropic organizations, similar to the ARA (American Relief Administration), disburse goods in the large cities. Demonstrations and strikes occur spontaneously. The same problems plague Yeltsin as Lenin: hyper-inflation, civil war in the provinces, unemployment, hoarding by peasant farmers.

Russia has come full circle. The circle encompasses a vast tragedy played out through the decades of the twentieth century. The loss of human life alone, in the wars and camps and famines, totals in the tens of millions. "Limbo" is how Aleksandr Solzhenitsyn described this sad condition in his novel *The First Circle*.

If Lenin attempted to learn the name of the system in this new Russia from a passerby on the street, he would likely be given the new acronym MASI: a mixture of alcoholism, socialism and idiotism. The slogan of the workers in the 20's, "We have nothing to lose but our chains," has been adapted in the new Russia: "We have nothing to lose but our place in line."

Following up on this curious response, Lenin might well ask, "And who is the leader of this new Russia?" "Yeltsin." "And who is Yeltsin?"

Boris Yeltsin

60-year-old Siberian. Protege of former Soviet President Mikhail Gorbachev and a member of the Communist Party's ruling Politburo until 1987, when he was ousted after attacking what he considered the slow pace of Gorbachev's reforms. He made a political comeback in popular elections to the National Congress of People's Deputies in 1989. He become Russia's first popularly elected president in June 1991. He led the opposition to August's hard-line coup attempt and became the moving force behind the formation of the new Commonwealth of Independent States, that formally replaced the USSR on December 18, 1991. While the leaders of the hard-line coup attempt were unable to coerce Gorbachev's resignation, Yeltsin forced his former mentor to step down on December 25, 1991.

The Problems

The basic problems facing Yeltsin are no different than those faced by every other Russian leader. But unlike Gorbachev, for example, who, in the beginning at least, had time on his side, real authority, and state and government bodies through which he could control the situation, Yeltsin has little to work with.

The shortages of food in the large cities are reminiscent of the situation during the Civil and Great Patriotic wars. The collective farms and peasants sabotage the traditional socialist policy of turning over their produce to the state. If they bring it to market at all, they demand a high price. Angry consumers today say that Stalin was right when he sent half of the kulak farmers to the camps in the thirties.

The communist leaders from Lenin onward solved the problem of shortages in two ways. First, they removed the produce from the villages by force. Second, they bought food from the West with hard currency earned from the sale of oil and gold. The new Russia has practically no hard currency or gold reserves. Planes have been grounded for lack of fuel. Strikes, lack of incentive, out-dated technology have cut the production of fuel by 20 percent. For now leaders have not resorted to the confiscation of agricultural products by force, but this cannot be ruled out in the future.

There is a Russian joke about the traditional communist approach. A new manager of a collective farm finds two letters from his predecessor, with instructions to open the first when difficulties begin. When the farm fails to meet its quotas, the manager opens the first letter which says "Blame me." He does. It buys some time. But the farm fails again, and he opens the second letter. It says: "Prepare two letters for your successor." If Yeltsin chooses the traditional approach, in a couple of months he will write two letters.

Russia very soon will have entered a revolutionary situation as defined by Lenin: when the authorities can no longer resolve accumulating political and economic problems and the people can no longer tolerate the aggravating crisis. The situation will resemble that of the summer of 1917, when the old managerial structures of the tsar's government were already dismantled, but the new structures of the Provisional Government as yet were unformed.

In fact, the country's managerial structures have been dismantled with the closing of the CPSU (Communist Party of the Soviet Union) committees at all levels.

Only the inertia of the Russian giant still keeps power plants operating and railway trains moving, although fuel reserves will dramatically dwindle (some of the country's power plants already have as little as 50-80 percent of the required amount of fuel oil). Supplies of goods and foodstuffs amount to only 70 percent of last year's level. Cheese and other delicacies are now remembered only by people with a terrific memory for the "good old days" of communist rule.

Russia will soon recall its tradition of revolts, sparked by hungry people craving bread. The driving force of the revolts will initially have a pronounced "female component", with women showing particular aggressiveness, attacking cooperative and private shops. The authorities will try to defuse the mounting social tension by using national gold reserves to buy food in the West. But Russian gold reserves now total only 250 tons. (In 1953 the USSR had record gold reserves of 2,049 tons).

In addition, the situation of ethnic Russians residing in the newly independent states will inevitably worsen, particularly in the Muslim states with their drive toward another Islamic revolution.

Yeltsin finds himself in a no win situation over the nationality question. He will be either accused of betraying the interests of Russians, or -- if he makes it understood that he will not oppose the "renaissance of Russian awareness" -- he will be branded a nationalist. According to an opinion poll carried out on August 20 (the day of the communist coup against Gorbachev), the Russian population supported Yeltsin the man, rather than the ideas of freedom and democracy.

For now, the regular army will rise up in support of the Russians. It will be confronted by local national-guard formations. The army has already virtually been abandoned to the mercy of fate in many regions and has to earn its livelihood on its own by sending trucks of soldiers to potato fields. As estimated by the Military-Political Department of the Institute of US and Canada, the army is barely controllable even now. With the old Union center dead, the new Russia has not yet learned to issue orders and authority. The new States, whose new economic condition is lamentable, are not at all eager to feed five million armed people who are seen in numerous regions as an occupation army.

The military-industrial complex (MIC), which employs as many as 11,400,000 persons, shares many of the army's problems. It stands only to lose with the new policies of disarmament and free market economy.

Soviet business is not currently in a position to play any significant role in the salvation of the new Russia. What most foreigners expect to see at Russian enterprises is antiquated machinery and men sitting around reading newspapers and drinking vodka. It is not quite true... There are also some women. Only a few Russian enterprises are self-sufficient.

The government has financed the black market, corruption and the mafia by subsidizing product prices and not controlling their distribution. The illegal gold traffic in the former USSR is now controlled by seven mafia groups. Incidentally, almost no conflict arises between these groups since there is so much stolen gold available (more than a ton annually). Clothing, food, liquor, entertainment and transportation, to name but a few, are sold on the black market. Many items can only be purchased unofficially and illegally at markets where shop managers do not even put the premium items on the shelf.

Lawmakers and enforcers would prefer a bribe in their pocket to the satisfaction of seeing their country's economy prosper. They conspire to deprive fellow-citizens of many goods which will be provided from the West. Furthermore, unreasonable taxes and constraints on private Russian businesses force many entrepreneurs to make deals under the table and through barter. Most state and private managers have little interest in cultivating their own market. Their preference is to sell goods abroad to earn hard currency and foreign travel. Many Russian enterprises barter with each other to provide their employees with scarce foods. The Soviet consumer is the clear loser.

BRIBES AS A PERCENTAGE OF PROFITS IN THE ECONOMY

Businesses	Profits in billions of roubles	Bribes paid in billions of roubles	Percentage
Transport	5.1	2.6	52
Retail Trade	8.8	4.9	56
Gambling and massage parlors	6.7	2.6	38

Only foreign assistance can steer the economy back on course and defuse a Russian Superbomb. This opinion is shared by economists as well as consumers in Russia. Four reasons obligate us to help Russia:

1. humanitarian considerations;
2. the diminished, but still real danger of nuclear war;
3. the possibility of civil war, which would cost us more in the long run;
4. the economic implications of a vast untapped market. No other country presents comparable long-term opportunities to be a major player in such a massive market.

Students in my Contemporary Russian Society class, created the following assistance models as part of their final assignment.

The U.N. Model

The U.N. has the obligation to help the newborn states to formulate their relations inside the Commonwealth, and should send teams to monitor issues of nuclear weapons control, humanitarian aid and ethnic conflict.

The Economic Development Model

1. Russia must drop all vestiges of communism and the command economy and allow the free market system to be adopted on Russian soil and by Russian souls;
2. Russian borders must be opened to foreign investors, farmers, and entrepreneurs;
3. Break up collective farms and allow private ownership of land;
4. Establish lending institutions to make small loans to businessmen and farmers;
5. Establish a fair method of taxation;
6. Organize a small professional army; provide retraining for personnel reentering civilian life.

The Foreign Aid Model

American and foreign aid should be spent mostly to send teams of consultants to help:

1. Set up community centers to solve immediate crises of food and medical supplies shortage;
2. Establish methods for collecting, storing and distributing agriculture products;
3. Provide life skills education to the Russian public to help in the transition to a market economy;
4. Consult on purchasing, setting up and running private businesses.

But the main goal of American aid must be to promote a new middle class which disappeared during the 74 years of communist rule. At the time of the French Revolution it was said that it is not difficult to proclaim a republic - but where do we get the republicans from? A new value system must be encouraged so that the new Russian man will support neither Yeltsin nor a new Lenin, but rather the ideas of democracy and a free society. The task is extremely difficult, and there is much to be done. But we must always bear in mind that Russia is a land where everything is forbidden, but nothing is impossible!

Chapter 13

Speech Is Free, Audience Is Extra

(Getting Invited To Speak)

"Hey. this is fun!" I thought to myself after surviving my first few presentations. "People pay me to tell them about Russia, a subject I can talk about all day, and they even laugh at my jokes." Just as Walter Cronkite predicted, I had found my new career in a country that offered just what I needed to succeed: freedom of speech.

In the United States, speech is free but speeches are not, at least not if the speaker wants to support a wife and daughter. Now all I needed were two things -- lots of practice and more audiences to address.

Reputation

My wife helped me with the first part and of course I got better as I tried out new jokes and ideas. But I didn't know where to start on the second part. Fortunately my reputation as "The Toilet Speaker" helped me get my foot in the door with different kinds of groups. Word of mouth advertising is valuable whenever you can get it, although I was surprised by the words peoples' mouths used to describe me. "He's a funny guy," they would say to endorse me to their friends. They never said, "He's brilliant and insightful." It was my use of humor and stories to entertain that made me a 'good speaker' in their eyes.

The Search

I started my search for new audiences by asking the people who invited me if they knew any other organizations that would enjoy hearing me speak. Then one day I told my wife I was going to drive around town looking for churches and schools where I might speak. "They are easy to find, since the buildings are so big," I said.

"You don't need to drive around town," she replied. "Just let your fingers walk through the yellow pages."

In Russian, the "yellow" pages or magazines refer to pornography, so I was shocked at my wife's suggestion. "No," she explained, "these yellow pages are part of the phone book. You can call those places instead of driving to them."

This was a suprise to me. In the Soviet Union they print very primitive telephone books, and then only every five years.

Why don't people in Russia need telephones? Because telephone books aren't available, and it's impossible to order pizza.

So I searched through the telephone book for groups I could address. Then I called them up and asked to speak to the program director or the person who arranges for speakers. I recommend calling first and talking with this person before you send any printed information about yourself.

Letters

If the program directors sounded even half-way interested, I drafted a letter to them. I described my background, explained what I could speak about, and listed several people who had scheduled me to speak to their groups as references. It was a typewritten sheet that I copied and mailed out, and it didn't get much response. You have to remember these people hear from all kinds of speakers and performers, but a few of my letters paid off with offers to speak.

I updated this "prospecting" letter after getting suggestions from a man who operated a speakers bureau. I tried to spice it up by saying I had worked for CBS News, was helped in my quest to emigrate by Congressman Foley, and that I would speak on topics like 'What Russian women do at night' and 'How you can win a million dollars.' I also added a list of organizations and schools where I had given presentations.

Flyers

After you mail out letters, the next level of sophistication is a one-page flyer. I had a picture taken of me with symbols of Russia (a big hat, a tea samovar and a picture of St. Basil's Cathedral) and of my new home in America (a baseball bat and an apple). I added a simple title ("Matvei Finkel presents A Personal View of Gorbachev's Russia") and a brief paragraph describing my presentation and how to contact me, and printed it up at a Quik Print. The flyer showed people what I looked like, and it gave me something to post on bulletin boards as free advertising.

Brochures

As my visibility as a speaker increased, I found myself wishing for something nicer and more informative to give to people when I was selling myself as a speaker. So I put together a very basic three-panel, folded brochure -- a couple of paragraphs about me, several jokes, and a few endorsements. I found someone to typeset and paste up the words with a couple of photos, I printed several hundred copies, and in just a little more time than it takes to tell, I was holding a sales brochure for the hottest commodity west of the rapidly rusting Iron Curtain: me.

I also revised my brochure several times, and I settled on several features that seem to make it an effective sales piece. First, put a good photo on the cover to catch the program director's attention. Include several lines on your background and qualifications to speak on your subject, and use the back of the piece to make your final pitch for why they should ask you to speak.

What should it look like? I looked at brochures from other speakers and then worked with a designer to prepare the artwork. We settled on a look that is simple and inexpensive, without looking cheap. I had it printed in one color, a dark blue, and used different percentage screens of blue as background shadings on some panels and to highlight information in a few boxes. Then I searched for a inexpensive printer and had her run off my piece, the current version of which is displayed in this section. The lady who printed them did a good job without costing me too many dollars. In fact, she was so inexpensive, she went bankrupt shortly after running it for me.

Recommendations

Another valuable sales piece is a letter of recommendation or appreciation. When people really enjoyed my presentation, I would ask the program director to write a letter to the chair of the modern languages department at Whitworth College where I teach classes. The best of these letters I copy and include in the materials I mail to program directors as a testimonial from a satisfied customer.

Contracts

When these phone calls and mailings get someone interested in having me speak, I ask for as much information as I can get. Things like the amount of the honorarium (my fee) and when I will receive it, type of overnight accomodations, reimbursement for mileage, type of audience, how many times I will speak and for how long. I mark it all on my schedule and send them an engagement contract form to seal the deal.

Work closely with the program director to get your questions answered before you finalize the contract. That way you can concentrate on your presentation, give them their money's worth, and have them begging you to come back again.

Chapter 14

From Russia With More Jokes

When I came to the United States, I was surprised to find that everything that happened in the Soviet Union had already been described by George Orwell in his writings. Orwell called political jokes "tiny revolutions," and maybe this is why his works were forbidden in Russia until last year.

With this chapter, you can organize your own tiny revolutions and not only will your audience survive, but they will reward you for it.

Communism

Some leaders in democratic countries are keen on collecting jokes about themselves. Russian leaders were keen on collecting the people who told them. Brezhnev was furious with the joke tellers: "It's a disgrace! Who makes them up? Bring me just one joke writer!" So they brought a joke writer to him. "How do you make up these jokes?" asked Brezhnev. The joke writer looked around with great admiration and said, "You don't live too badly." "In twenty years we'll have true Communism and everybody will live like this!" said Brezhnev. "Aha!" says the writer. "A new joke."

A Russian disadent trying to escape from the Soviet Union was caught and interrogated by the KGB. "Why were you trying to leave?" asked the officer. "Because," said the disadent, "if the government ever fell, I would be blamed." "You are a fool," laughed the officer, "the government will never fall" To which the dissadent replied, "That brings me to the second reason I'd like to leave the Soviet Union..."

A boy asks, "What will communism be like when it is perfected?" His father replies, "Everyone will have what he needs." The boy asks, "But what if there is a shortage of meat." The father replies, "There will be a sign in the butcher shop saying, 'No one needs meat today.'"

The presiding officer was addressing a man who was about to join the Russian Communist Party. Suppose somebody died and you were bequeathed 10,000 rubles -- what would you do? "I would give 5,000 to the Party and keep the other five for myself," said the man. "Very good," said the officer. "And now, supposing you had two pair of pants." The candidate hesitated. "Sir," he finally stammered, "I don't think that question is fair. I happen to have two pair of pants!"

What are the four stages of Socialism? Utopian Socialism, Scientific Socialism, Real Socialism and a Coup.

Socialism in Russia is the synthesis of the stages of mankind's developments. From pre-history it takes its methods. From antiquity, it takes slavery. From feudalism, serfdom. From capitalism, exploitation. From socialism, it only borrowed the name.

The five rules of Socialism: Don't think. If you do think, don't speak. If you do speak, don't write. If you think, speak and write, don't sign. And if you think, speak, write and sign, don't be surprised.

What is the difference between a Materialist, an Idealist and a Marxist? A Materialist is in a dark room, chasing a non-existent black cat and he knows there is no cat. An Idealist is in a dark room, chasing a non-existent black cat and he believes there is a cat. A Marxist is in a dark room, chasing a non-existent black cat, and he keeps finding it.

"I have so much freedom," said an American, "I can go to the White House and complain about the president." "Well I can go to the Kremlin," said a Russian, "and complain about your president, too."

I had a very nice full length leather coat in the Soviet Union, but when I came to America I discovered it only reached to the middle of my thighs. "In Moscow, this was a full length coat," I complained to my wife. "When you were in Moscow," she reminded me, "you were on your knees."

What is the difference between a Christian and a Communist? A Christian believes in life after death. A Communist believes in rehabilitation after death.

What is a Soviet string trio? A Soviet string quartet returning from an overseas tour.

The Soviet defense minister visited a small European country and was introduced to its minister of defense. "Whatever do you do?" the Soviet asked with a chuckle. "There is nothing here to defend." "Sir," replied the minister, "I am insulted. When I visited Moscow and was introduced to your minister of justice, at least I contained my laughter."

Economics

A teacher was explaining to a Russian kindergarten class how the Soviet Union had everything. "There is plenty of food, nice clothes, nice apartments, and," she added with a smile, "there is always candy for the children to eat." At that, one of her pupils began to cry. "I want to go to the Soviet Union!" he said.

"In Russia, the people pretend to work and the government pretends to pay them."

A friend of mine wanted to visit Russia. "Hotels are very cheap in Russia, only about three dollars a night," I told him, "but you have to make your own bed." "What's so bad about that?" asked my friend. "They give you a hammer, some nails and an armload of two-by-fours," I replied.

A Russian immigrant to America came home from his first day of work and described his new job to his wife. "I work on an assembly line with three other fellows," said the man. "A car comes down the line, the first guy puts on the bolt, the second ties the washers, and the third holds the bolt and washers in place." "And what do you do?" asked his wife. "Me? I screw up the works," he replied.

It is much easier to buy a house in California than in Russia. You only need three things: a real estate agent, a lawyer, and a winning lottery ticket.

In America we have nearly all of the world's cars. So how come the Russians got all the parking spaces?

Business, Russian style: Petya and Vasya stole a case of vodka from a distillery, took it to the market and sold it. Then they spent the money getting drunk.

A Soviet teacher asked his class to compare their country to the United States. "They have eight million unemployed," a student replied, "and 100,000 homeless people." "Very good," said the teacher. "And what is the goal of the Soviet Union?" he asked. "To catch up to the United States," another student answered.

Why don't Russian workers ever go on strike? Because no one would notice the difference.

Militarism And The K.G.B.

Referring to Soviet invasions of Hungary, Czechoslovakia, Afghanistan: The Soviet Union recognized international boundaries, although you must remember that Soviet friendship knew no boundaries. What countries did the Soviet Union border? Any countries it wished to border.

Inside Sweden people drive Saabs, and outside the country they drive Volvos. Inside the Soviet Union people drive tractors, and outside the country they drive tanks.

To understand what the Soviet secret police was like, try combining the F.B.I., the C.I.A., the national guard, the immigration service and the I.R.S.

What's the biggest difference between an American circus and the KGB? In a circus you have to pay money to watch them saw women in half and make people disappear. The KGB performed the same tricks for free.

Two Russian brothers living in America wanted to visit their mother in Moscow, but they were afraid of the KGB. One agreed to go and write back using red ink if it was dangerous for the other to come. Soon the one in America received a letter from his brother that said everything was wonderful in the Soviet Union. The only problem, the letter said, was he couldn't find any red ink.

A Russian was arrested by the Soviet secret police when they found American matches in his possession. He told the judge he was using Capitalistic matches, but only to light People's matches.

An American spy was ordered by the CIA to go to Russia and make contact with another CIA spy named Ivanov. He had memorized Ivanov's address, but when he reached the building's hallway he found not one but two Ivanovs listed. So he tried ringing the doorbell of the first one. "Are you Ivanov?" "Yes." "Are you going to Siberia?" asked the American agent, giving the password. "Oh, no!" said the man. "I am Ivanov the driver. You want Ivanov the spy -- he is on the third floor!"

"What are you in for?" one prisoner asks another. "I was lazy," he explained. "I was having a chat with a friend of mine about the political situation, and I thought I could wait until morning before denouncing him. He managed to get to the Security Police the same night."

After I came to the United States, I ran in a very large race. When people asked me how I managed to run so fast, I told them I thought the people behind me were KGB agents in disguise, and that all 50,000 people in the race were running to buy one chicken.

Why do Russians run so fast in the Olympics? Because their coaches have real bullets in the starting guns.

Gorbachev

The Soviet Union was a one-man one-vote country. The one man was Gorbachev and he had the one vote.

"Do you want to hear the latest joke about Gorbachev," one man asked another. "Yes," said the second man, "but you have to know I'm working for Gorbachev." "That's okay," said the first man. "I'll tell it very slowly."

Four years ago, I wrote, "I wonder, would Gorbachev be tempted to defect to America? We would have to make room for one more lawyer, and surely we have enough of them already."

Ted Kennedy says to Michail Gorbachev, "The difference between you and me is that I came to power from the privileged class, whereas you came to power from the peasant class." Gorbachev replies, "That is true. But there is this similarity. Each of us is a traitor to his class."

Democratic Party leaders in the U.S. wanted to invite Gorbachev to be a presidential candidate in the next presidential elections. "We need you, Mr. Gorbachev," they said. "You are a man with charisma, who has a photogenic wife and can handle hard-liners." Gorbachev replied, "I thank you for your invitation, but I cannot accept -- for ideological reasons. Not because I am a Communist. It's just that I'm a Republican."

Russian proverb: "Gorbachev gave us the truth, the whole truth, but nothing else."

Vodka

There are only three different kinds of cocktails in Russia. One glass of vodka, two glasses of vodka, and a bottle of vodka.

Refering to vodka's role in Soviet life: Between capitalism and communism lies a long period of socialism. Between socialism and communism lies an even longer period of alcoholism.

After Gorbachev's anti-drinking campaign, a bureaucrat was trying to get romantic with his new secretary. The lady was willing but wanted to close the office door. "Please don't close it," begged the bureaucrat. "People will think we are having a drink."

When Gorbachev visited Washington D.C., he complained that Russians had a reputation for drinking. "I'm sure Americans like to drink even more than Russians," he said, so his hosts gave him a revolver and permission to kill the first fifty people he saw walking down the street who were drunk. Gorbachev proceeded to kill his quota of drunks in the first night. The next morning the headlines read: "Bald Russian Gunman Kills 50 Employees of Soviet Embassy!"

An American and a Russian were arguing over who had the most ambitious leader. "My award goes to Herbert Hoover, who tried to teach Americans to stop drinking," said the American. "That's nothing," said the Russian. "I pick Gorbachev. He tried to teach Russians to stop eating."

Shortages

When you see someone running in Russia, the first thing everyone wants to know is what kind of food they are running to buy.

An American interviewed Russians standing in a line to buy food. "Excuse me," he said, "what is your opinion of the shortage of meat in Russia?" The first person asked "What's the meaning of 'meat'?" The second person asked "What's the meaning of 'opinion'?" The third person asked "What's the meaning of 'excuse me'?"

What is 450 yards long and eats potatoes? A Moscow queue waiting to buy meat.

The shortages in Russia are so severe, visiting a friend can involve difficult choices. "Do you want sugar with your tea or would you like to wash your hands with soap?" asks the host. "Take your pick."

Until recently, Russian schools taught Atheism as a primary subject, but shortages of food has become a more important topic of discussion. A teacher was reading a fable to children. "...and God gave the raven a piece of cheese." A small boy jumped to his feet and protested: "There is no such thing as cheese!"

Russian proverb: "It's easier to make a pot of fish soup from a bowl of live fish, than to make a bowl of live fish from a pot of fish soup."

"I see you have no vegetables here," a Russian woman told the man behind an empty counter. "That's not true," said the man. "We sell bread here, and we have no bread. The shop with no vegetables is around the corner."

A customer asked a Russian storeowner, "Do you have a scale?" "Yes, I do," he replied. "But," the customer asked, "do you have any food?"

A man asked a little Russian girl about her parents. "Nobody's home," she said. "When will your father be back?" he asked. "In eight hours, 37 minutes, 23 seconds," she replied. "How do you know for sure?" "Because he is a cosmonaut, and that is when he will land." "Well, when will your mother be back?" he asked. "I don't know," she said. "What does she do?" he inquired. "She went to find some bread," the girl replied.

"Adam and Eve must have been Russians. Who else could be naked, have only one apple to eat and still think they were in paradise?"

A Russian met an American near the gates of heaven and discovered they both were killed by their cars. The American died when he drove too fast and blew a tire. The Russian tried to save money to buy a car and died of starvation.

Five years ago, the Russians planned to build the biggest supermarket in the world and hire 150 people to run it. They just finished it, but they only hired two people to work there. One employee stands at the entrance saying "Nothing to buy," while the other stands at the exit and says, "Now are you convinced?"

In the future, meat will be supplied jointly by the Americans and the Russians. Americans will supply the meat. Russians will supply the rationing coupons.

The Moscow Exhibition of Economic Achievements recently held a show entitled "The Exhibit of Poor Quality Goods." The display featured dresses with uneven sleeves, bread with nails in it, and a bottle of mineral water containing a dead mouse. One exhibit goer said, "This isn't so bad. Most stores have nothing at all."

In Russia, a fly in your soup is considered a two-course meal! Russian restaurants don't have waiters. Customers are the waiters -- always waiting for food. In America, you leave a tip. In Russia you just want to leave.

A Russian visitor to the U.S. says to his American host, "you must have terrible shortages." The astonished American asks why he thinks so. "Because you have no lines," the visitor replies.

A Moscovite asks her butcher for beef and is told there is none. She asks for chicken. "None." Lamb? "None." Pork? "None." The shopper leaves and the butcher's assistant exclaims to him, "She hasn't seen meat in years, but she still remembers what it's called. What a terrific memory!"

There's only one way to get water in a Russian restaurant -- set yourself on fire.

Yeltsin

Yeltsin solved the problem of the shortage of food. Now there's no food.

Yeltsin is told by his secretary that two visitors are waiting to see him. "Who are they?" he asks. "The Russian Patriarch and an American capitalist," he is told. "Show the Patriarch in first," Yeltsin says. "I only have to kiss his hand."

Yeltsin hands a coin to a beggar in New York. "Who are you?" asks the beggar. "I am the Russian President," replies Yeltsin. "Thank you," says the beggar, "but you can have this back. I don't take money from colleagues."

Yeltsin's mother came to visit her son. "This is my house, my car, and my swimming pool," he said. "Near the Black Sea I have a villa and a yacht." "You do very well my son," his mother said, "but I'm worried for you. What if the Communists come back?"

Yeltsin arrives at the Kremlin and decides to inspect all the offices. He opens one door and sees a woman reading "Pravda." He opens a second door and sees a man reading "Pravda." Yeltsin cries "Duplication! Both are reading Pravda."

In 1992 there will be an assasination attempt on the life of the Russian President Boris Yeltsin. A shot will be fired intended for Yeltsin but his chauffeur will be wounded. Why? Too many people will try to grab the pistol, shouting "Give it to me! Let me do it!" Either that, or the chauffeur will be wounded after the bullet ricochets off Yeltsin's head.

When Yeltsin came to power and occupied Gorbachev's office, his secretary found boxes full of Gorbachev's files. "What should I do with them?" he asked. "Throw them away," replied the President of Russia. "But don't forget to make a copy of each document first."

Yeltsin is Gorbachev, but with charisma.

The Free Market Blues

"Moving to a free market is like castor oil. Easy to recommend, but dreadful to have to take."

"In the new Russia, everyone will have strawberries and cream," says the politician. "But I don't like strawberries and cream," shouts a man in the audience. "In the new country," assures the politician, "you *will* like them."

The Russian finance minister went to the World Bank to get a loan. "For collateral, we have vast deposits of oil, gold and silver," he said. "But that is all underground," replied the bank official. "What do you have above ground?" "Well, we have superb Russian leaders." "I don't think we can give you a loan." said the bank official, "until the two groups trade places."

Russia has found a new way to get foreign currency. A new sign on the Kremlin says "McDonalds coming soon!"

After Yeltsin lifted price controls, two Russians met in a line. "Well Ivan," said one grimly, "do you think we have already reached 100 per cent socialism, or will it get worse?"

Russians who haved lived under a planned economy all their lives find it hard to adjust to free enterprise at first. After they were helped by Americans to set up shops, they started to call the American president to complain, "Why haven't you sent me any customers?"

A Russian barber keeps asking a man about the free market. Eventually, the man asks angrily: "Why are you so interested in a free market?" "Oh, I'm not," says the barber. "It's just that every time I mention it, your hair stands on end."

Russia is trying to convert military factories into ones that produce consumer goods. I think they ought to convert the tank factories into refrigerator factories -- they are both heavy, they look alike, and in Russia the refrigerators even sound like tanks.

Political Changes

A legislator from Latvia, which recently declared its independence from the Soviet Union, wanted to declare war on Russia. Another legislator screamed that he was crazy. "How can our small country fight against a military giant? We will certainly lose." "Remember that France, Germany and Japan all declared war against Russia and lost," said the first man. "Look how successful they are now." Everyone agreed with his reasoning, except for one legislator who asked, "But what would happen if we won?"

From the Soviet Union to Russia: A census official questions an elderly citizen of Leningrad in 1990. Where were you born? "St. Petersburg," he answers. Where were you educated? "Petrograd." Where do you live? "Leningrad." Where do you want to die? "St. Petersburg." Now it is no joke.

Russia 1992: What is black and knocking at the door? The Future.

Question: Will there be a civil war in Russia? Answer: No, but there will be such a struggle for peace that not one stone will be left standing.

daring DISCOVERY
artists & lectures 1991-92

Oct. 17, 1991
Ann Jillian

A Conversation With Ann Jillian

An intimate encounter with the award winning stage, screen, video actress and comedienne so much admired for her warmth, courage and humanitarian contributions.
Don't miss the Reception to follow!

Feb. 6, 1992
Dr. Joyce Brothers

Unlocking Your Hidden Power

Dynamic life therapy with a smile in this lively interaction with a favorite psychologist, author and TV personality extraordinaire.

The New Russia: A Waking Giant

A lively close-up on life in mother Russia by a former Red Army soldier, aerospace engineer and CBS news consultant, recently turned American citizen and college professor.

Mar. 12, 1992
Matvei Finkel

What's really going on in Russia?
Invite Matvei to speak to your group . . .
Russians will no longer be strangers to you.
(509) 922-0753

☐ Yes, we are interested.

Best date for us is _____

☐ No, we are not interested.

Organization

Name: _____

Address: _____

Programmer

Name: _____

Work Phone: _____

Home Phone: _____

Matvei Finkel was born in the USSR. For forty years he was a loyal Soviet citizen; he served in the Red Army and worked as an engineer, a teacher and a magazine editor. His marriage to an American woman provoked the wrath of Soviet officialdom.

For four years before he emigrated, Matvei worked as a consultant for CBS News in Moscow. He assisted Walter Cronkite, Mike Wallace and Diane Sawyer in the production of special programs about the Soviet Union.

Currently, Matvei teaches Russian language and culture at Whitworth College in Washington state and works as a consultant on Russian affairs.

To order Matvei Finkel's books and tapes, find out more about his presentations, or receive information on how you can help Russians in their transition to a democratic state and a free market, send a self-addressed envelope to Matvei Finkel at the following address:

N. 4908 Darin Rd., Otis Orchards, WA 99027.
(509) 922-0753

Question: "Who will be the next leader of Russia after Yeltsin?"
Answer: "I don't know his name, but he will be bald."